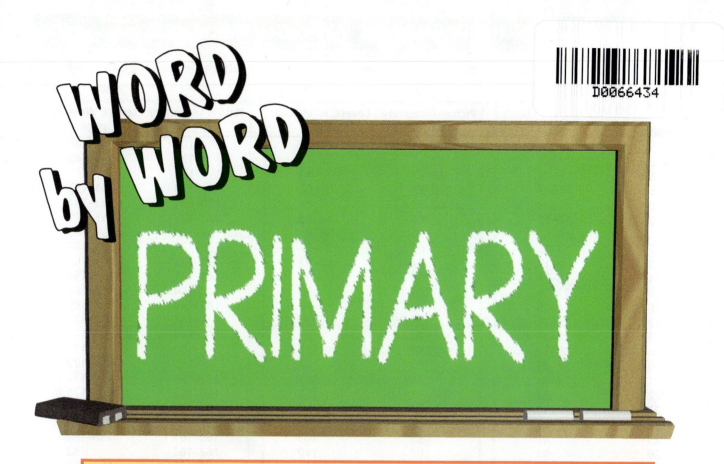

WORD by WORD

PRIMARY

LEVEL C PHONICS WORKBOOK

Steven J. Molinsky • Bill Bliss

Illustrated by

Richard E. Hill

Maya Shorr Katz

Longman

Picture Dictionary / Level C Workbook Correlation

This correlation indicates how the activity pages in this workbook coordinate with the lessons in the *Word by Word Primary Phonics Picture Dictionary*.

Picture Dictionary pages	Level C Workbook pages	Picture Dictionary pages	Level C Workbook pages	Picture Dictionary pages	Level C Workbook pages
2–3	1–2	51	75–76	126	148
4–5	3–4	52–55	77–79	127	149
6	5	56–57	80	128	150
8	6–7	58–59	81–82	129	151–152
9	8–9	60–62	83	130–131	153–154
10	10–11	64	84–85	132–133	155–158
11	12–13	65	86–87	134–135	159
12	14–15	66	88–89	136–137	160
13	16–17	67	90–93	138–139	161–162
14	18–21	68	94	140–141	163–164
15	22–23	69	95	142–144	165–167
16	24–25	70	96	146–147	168–169
17	26–27	71	97	148	170
18	28–29	72	98	149	171
19	30–31	73	99–101	150	172
20	32–33	74	102	151	173
21	34–37	75	103	152–153	174
22	38	76–77	104–105	154–155	175
23	39	78–79	106–107	156–157	176–177
24	40	80	108	158–159	178–179
25	41	81	109	160–161	180–182
26	42–43	82	110	162–163	183
27	44	83	111	164–165	184–186
28	45	84	112	166–167	187–188
29	46	85	113	168	189–190
30	47	86–87	114–115	169	191
31	48	88–89	116–118	170	192–193
32	49	90	119	171	194
33	50	91	120	172	195–198
34	51	92–95	121	173	199–200
35	52	96–97	122–123	174	201
36	53–54	98–99	124	175	202
37	55	100–101	125–126	176	203
38	56	102–103	127	177	204
39	57–58	104–105	128	178	205–206
40	59	106–107	129	180–181	207–208
41	60–61	108	130	182–183	209–211
42	62	110–111	131–132	184–185	212–214
43	63–64	112–113	133–134	186–187	215–217
44	65	114–115	135–136	188	218
45	66–67	116–117	137–138	189	219
46	68	118–119	139–140	190–191	220–221
47	69–70	120–121	141–142	192–193	222
48	71	122–123	143–145	194	223
49	72–73	124	146	195	224–225
50	74	125	147	196–197	226–227
				198–199	228–229

Word by Word Primary Phonics Level C Workbook
Copyright © 2001 by Addison Wesley Longman, Inc.

ISBN 0-13-022166-X

Printed in the United States of America

9   10   11   12   13

Pearson Education, 10 Bank St., White Plains, NY 10606

CONTENTS

Note: The symbol ← in this workbook indicates a word in the past tense.

Editorial Director: *Allen Ascher*
Executive Editor: *Anne Stribling*
Director of Design and Production: *Rhea Banker*
Associate Director of Electronic Publishing: *Aliza Greenblatt*
Production Manager: *Ray Keating*
Senior Manufacturing Manager: *Patrice Fraccio*

Manufacturing Buyer: *Edith Pullman*
Digital Layout Specialists, Page Compositors, Interior Designers: *Rachel Baumann–Weber, Paula D. Williams, Wendy Wolf*
Associate Art Director: *Ann France*
Cover Artists: *Richard E. Hill, Carey Davies*
Illustrations: *Richard E. Hill, Maya Shorr Katz*

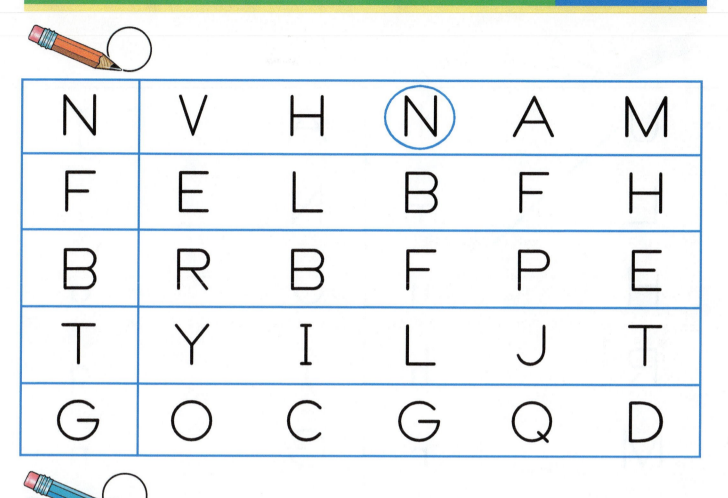

N	V	H	(N)	A	M
F	E	L	B	F	H
B	R	B	F	P	E
T	Y	I	L	J	T
G	O	C	G	Q	D

l	i	b	t	(l)	k
u	n	v	h	m	u
c	e	s	o	c	a
p	h	p	b	d	q
b	p	d	b	h	k

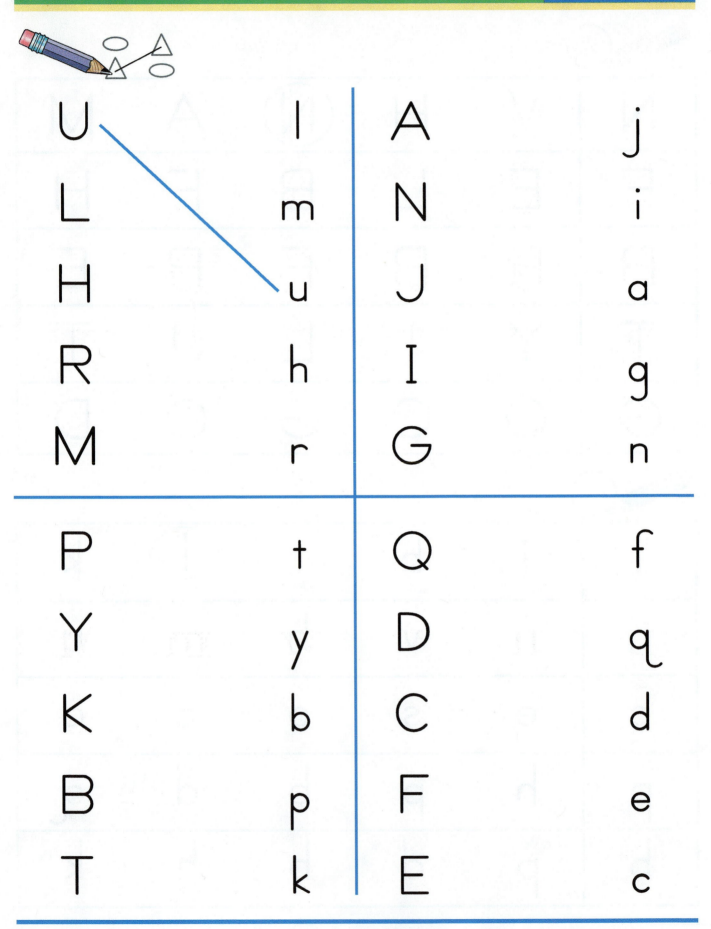

U	l	A	j
L	m	N	i
H	u	J	a
R	h	I	g
M	r	G	n
P	t	Q	f
Y	y	D	q
K	b	C	d
B	p	F	e
T	k	E	c

B	H	E	(B)	D	P
V	U	Y	W	A	V
O	Q	O	G	D	C
R	F	K	B	P	R
C	Q	G	C	D	O

i	(i)	t	j	h	l
n	u	v	w	m	n
e	c	o	e	a	s
b	h	d	p	b	q
q	p	b	d	q	h

J	g	H	y
G	r	D	i
R	t	I	h
T	a	M	d
A	j	Y	m
N	M	f	g
F	N	t	f
R	F	r	t
M	Z	g	a
Z	R	a	r

m (v)   m v   m v

van (man) (man) van

van   man   van   man

man   van   van   man

van	man	man	van	van	man
a man	a van	a van	a man		
a man in a van	a man in a van				

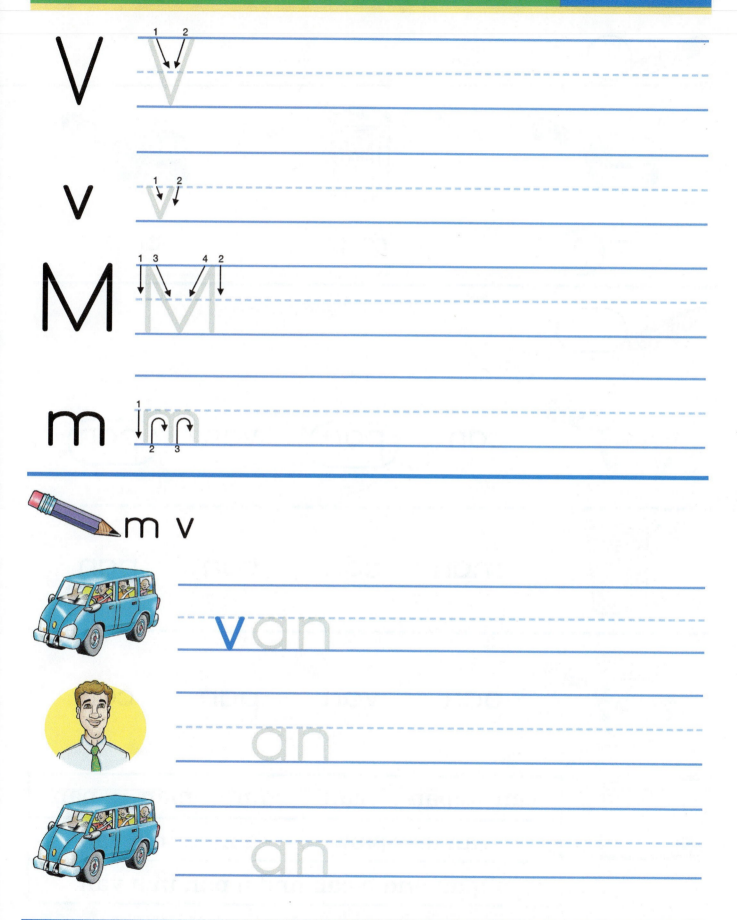

V

v

M

m

m v

van

man

van

c (p)   c p   c p

can   (pan)   van   (pan)

man   can   can   pan

pan   van   pan   can

can	pan	can	van	man	pan
a can in a pan			a man in a van		
a man and a can and a pan in a van					

m (b) c   m b c   m b c

bat   can   (cat)   van

mat   pan   pat   bat

man   mat   can   pan

cat	can	bat	pan	man	mat
a cat in a van			a bat in a van		
a man and a cat and a bat in a van					

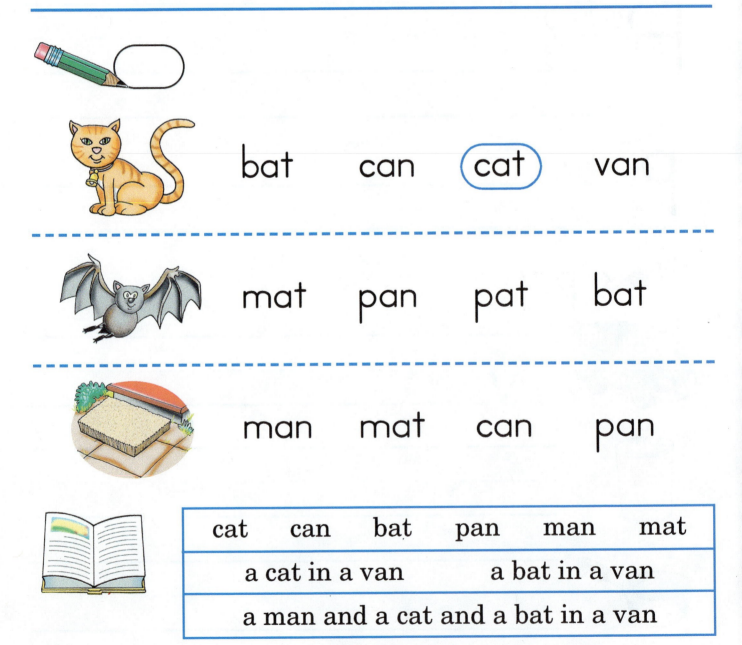

10

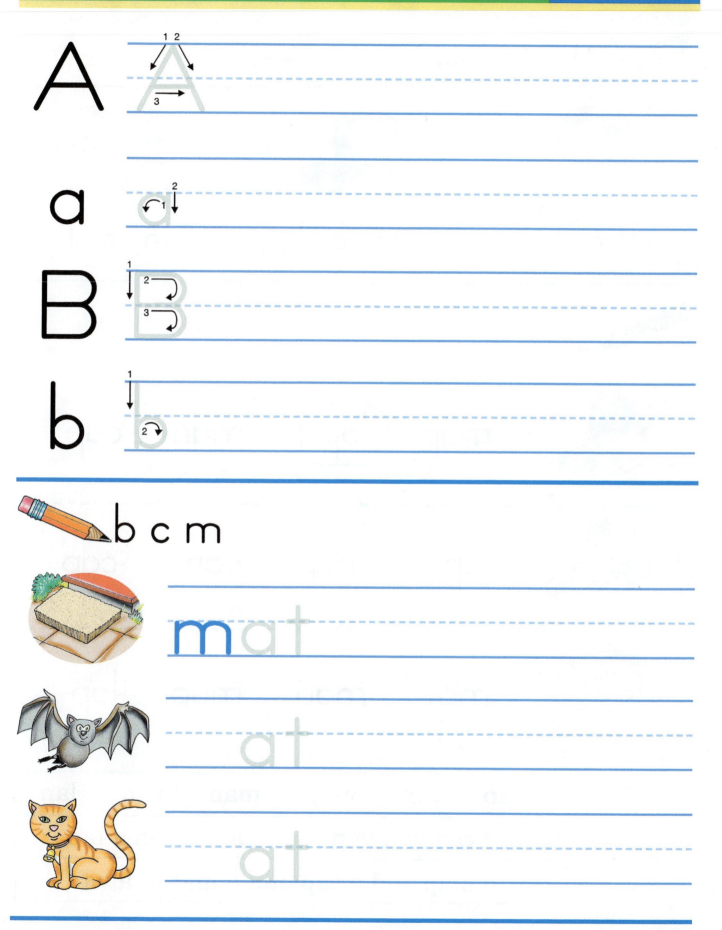

A A

a a

B B

b b

b c m

mat

at

at

m (c) l   m c l   m c l

map   (lap)   man   cap

lap   map   can   cap

mat   man   map   lap

cap	can	map	man	van	lap
a cap in a van			a map on a lap		
a map and a cap and a mat in a van					

L l

I l

M

m

c m l

cap

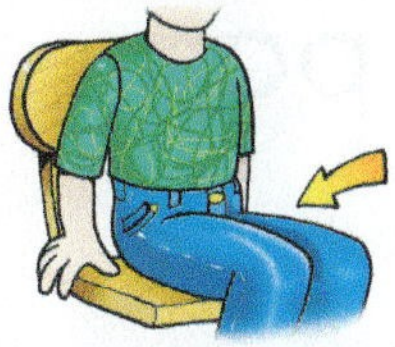

ap

ap

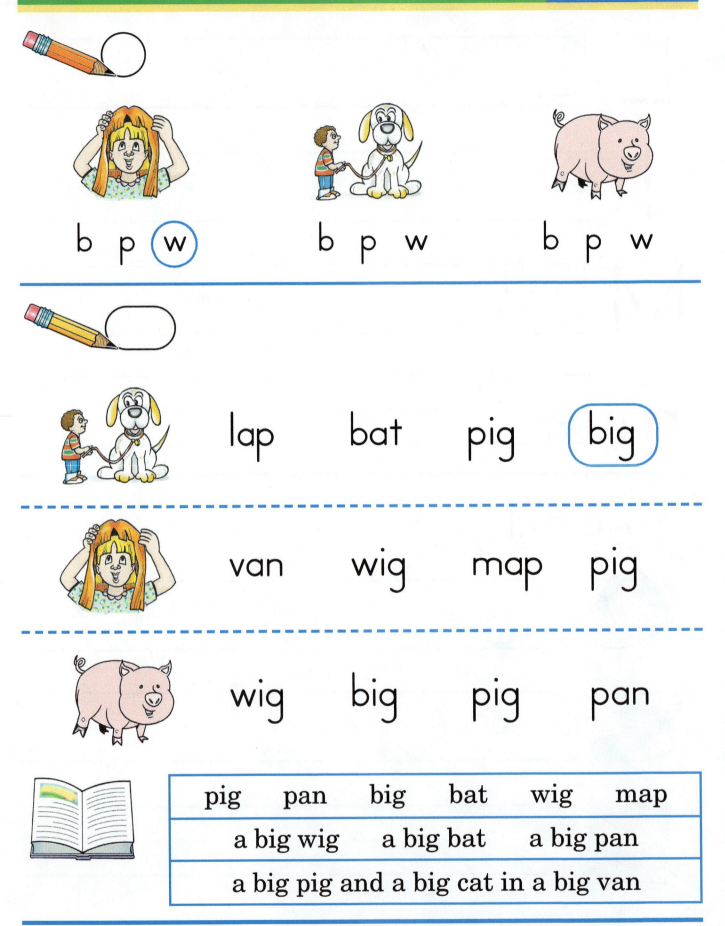

b p (w)　　　b p w　　　b p w

lap　　bat　　pig　　(big)

van　　wig　　map　　pig

wig　　big　　pig　　pan

pig	pan	big	bat	wig	map
a big wig		a big bat		a big pan	
a big pig and a big cat in a big van					

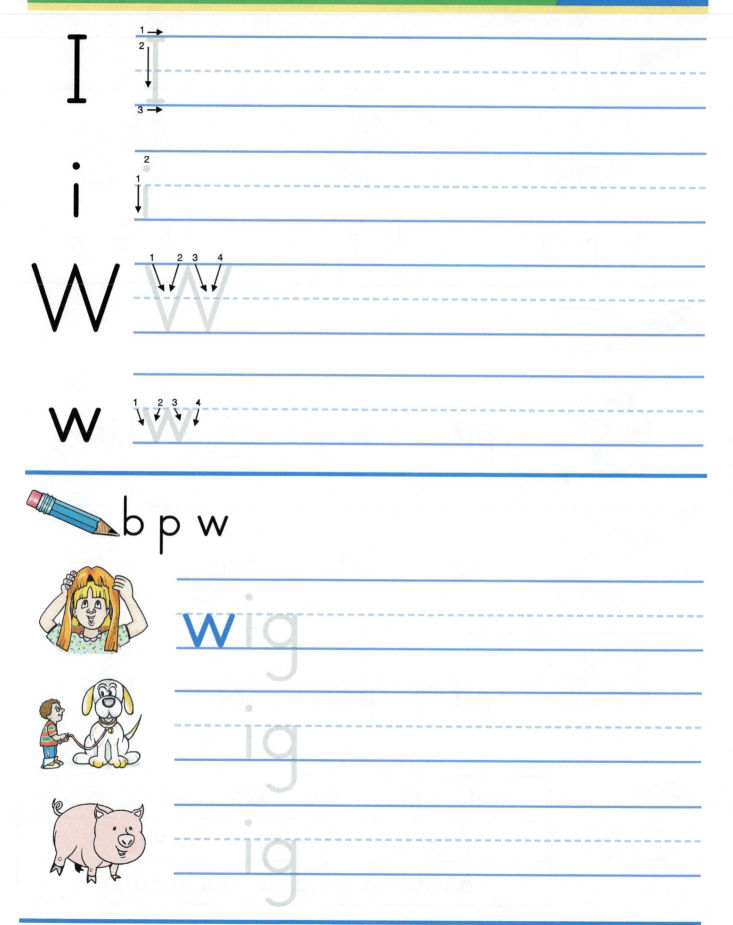

b p w

wig

ig

ig

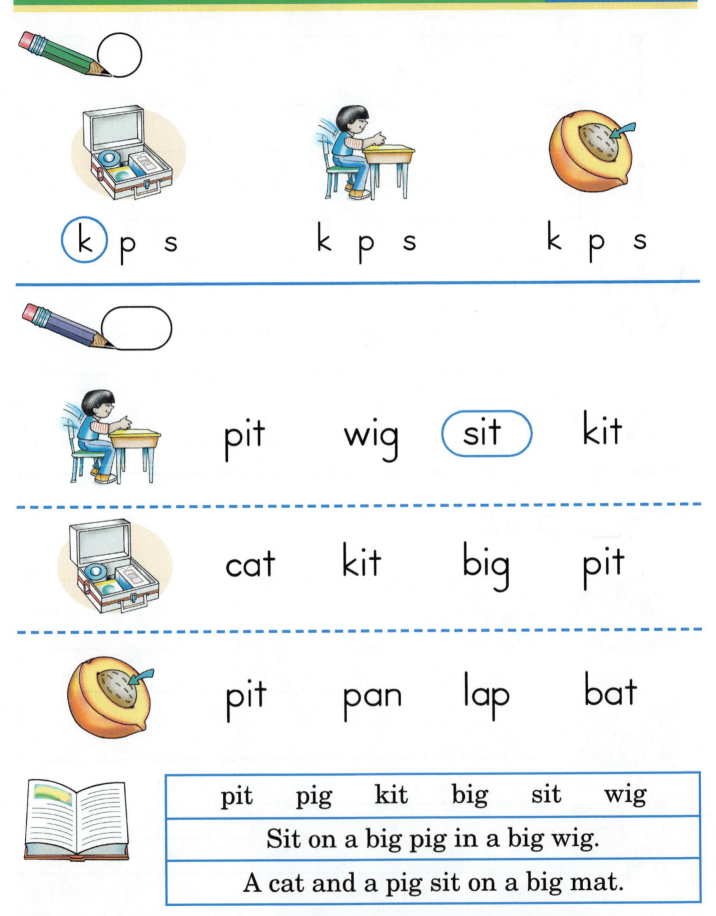

k p s   k p s   k p s

pit   wig   sit   kit

cat   kit   big   pit

pit   pan   lap   bat

pit	pig	kit	big	sit	wig

Sit on a big pig in a big wig.

A cat and a pig sit on a big mat.

K k

S s

k p s

pit

pit

pit

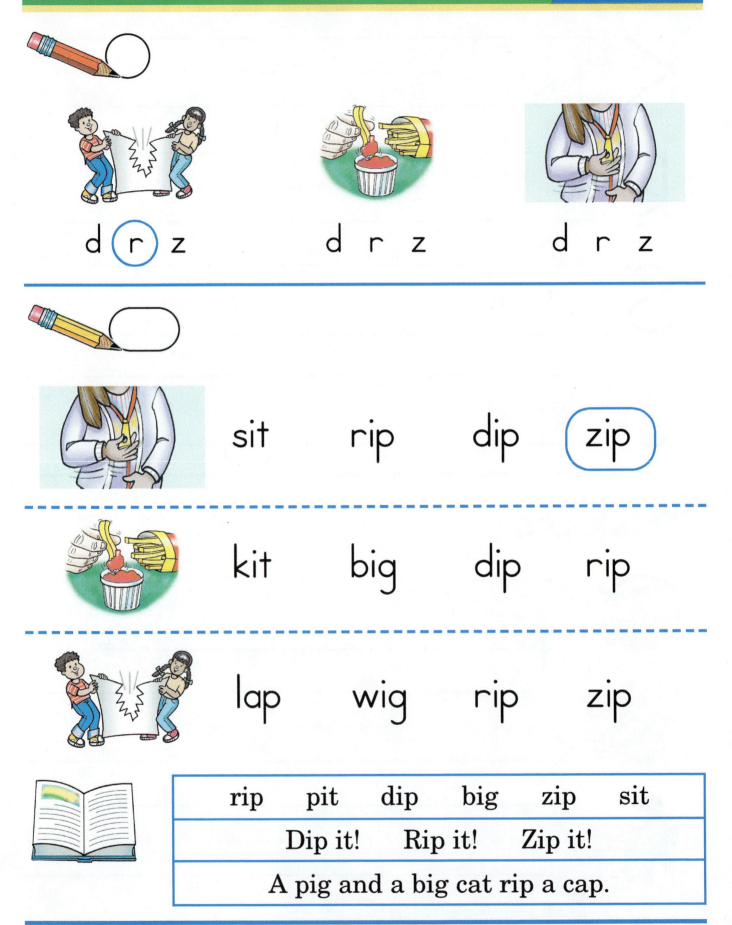

d (r) z   d r z   d r z

sit   rip   dip   (zip)

kit   big   dip   rip

lap   wig   rip   zip

rip   pit   dip   big   zip   sit

Dip it!   Rip it!   Zip it!

A pig and a big cat rip a cap.

1.

2.

3.

4.

5.

6.

w f p   w f p   w f p

pit   pig   pin   fin

fin   sit   wig   win

kit   fin   pin   win

pin	pit	pig	win	wig	fin

Win a pin.   Win a pan.   Win a van.

Win a wig and a big pin with a fin.

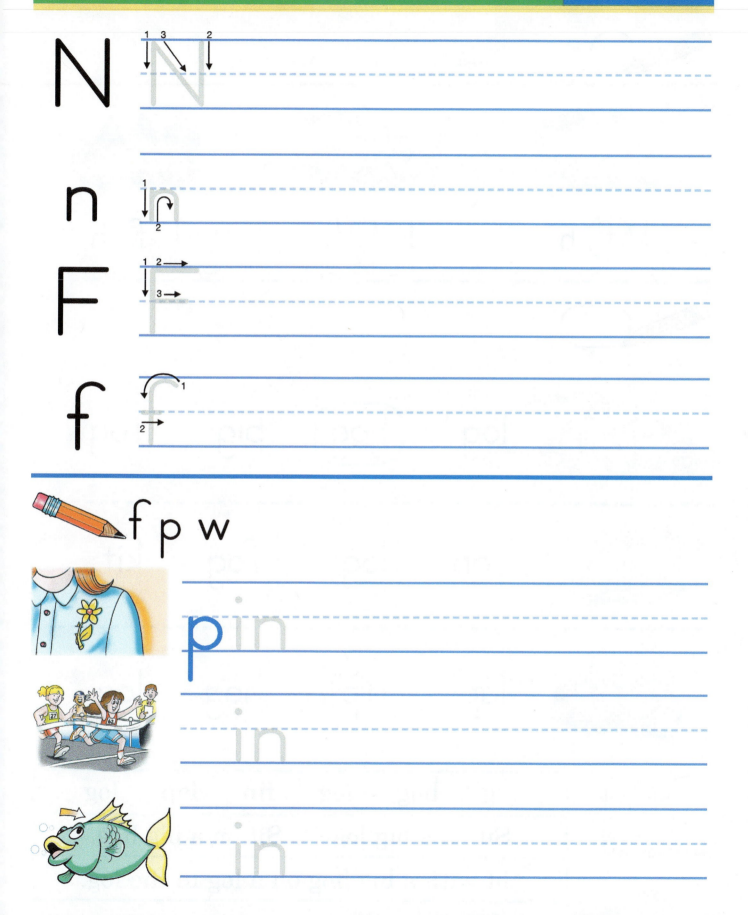

f p w

p in

in

in

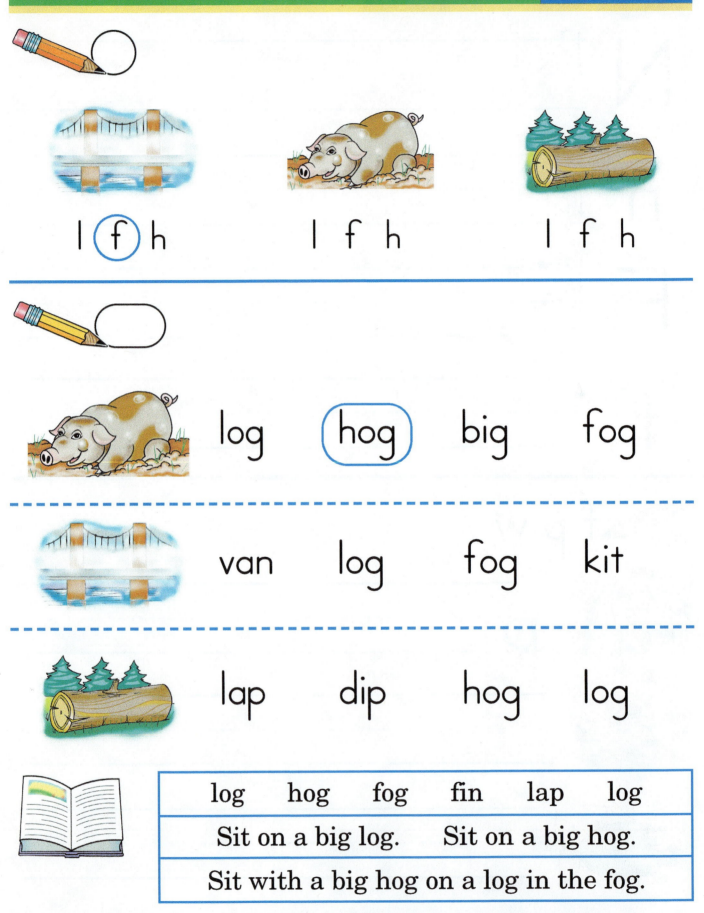

l (f) h   l f h   l f h

log   (hog)   big   fog

van   log   fog   kit

lap   dip   hog   log

| log | hog | fog | fin | lap | log |

Sit on a big log.   Sit on a big hog.

Sit with a big hog on a log in the fog.

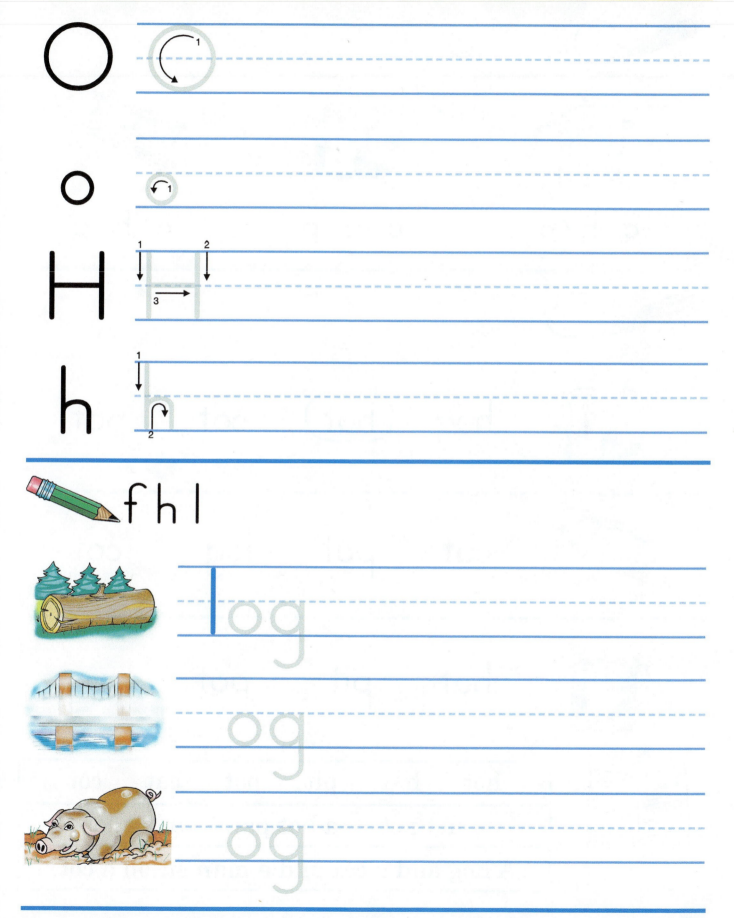

f h l

log

og

og

c h (p)   c h p   c h p

hog   (hot)   cot   pot

cat   pot   log   cot

hot   pit   pot   can

hot	hat	pit	pot	cat	cot
a hot pot		a hot pan		a big cot	
A hog and a cat and a man sit on a cot.					

b c h p s

c o t

o t

o t

i t

a t

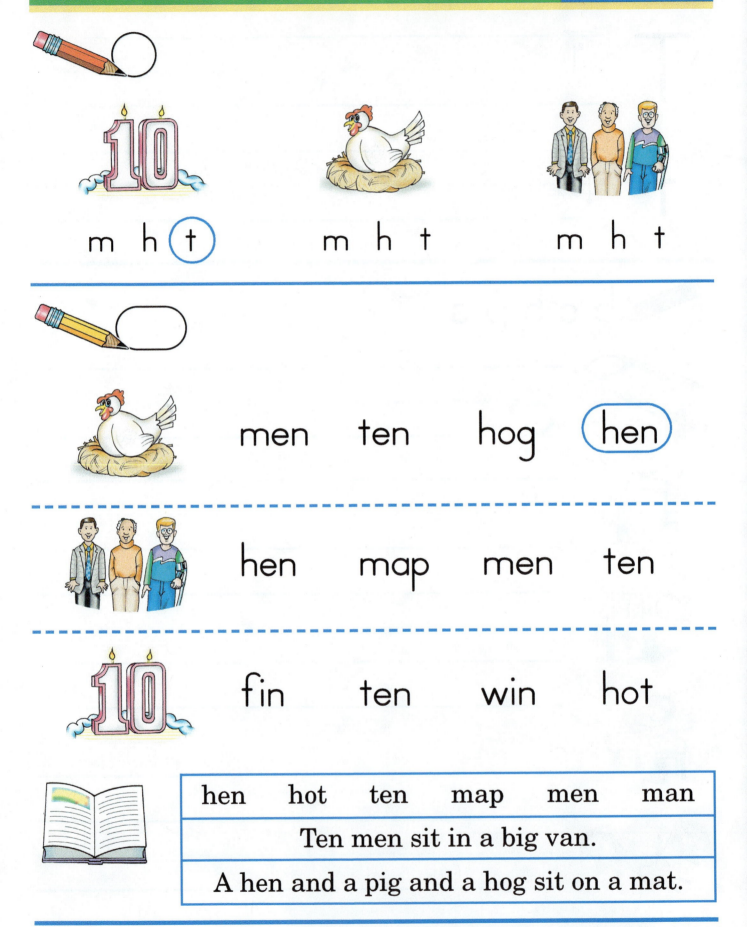

m   h   (t)   m   h   t   m   h   t

men   ten   hog   (hen)

hen   map   men   ten

fin   ten   win   hot

hen   hot   ten   map   men   man

Ten men sit in a big van.

A hen and a pig and a hog sit on a mat.

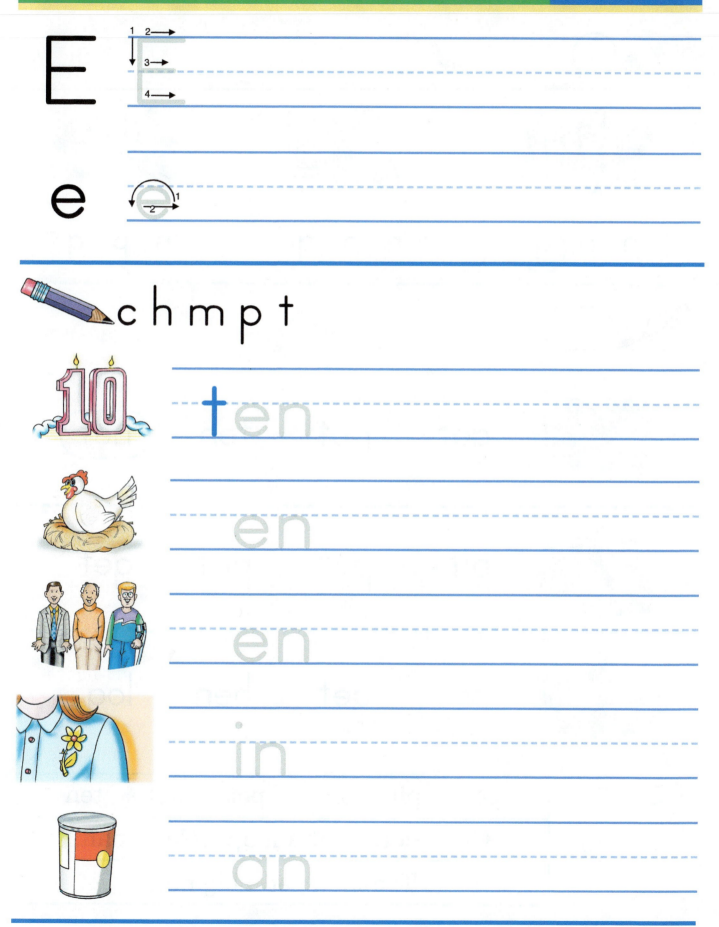

E

e

c h m p t

ten

en

en

in

an

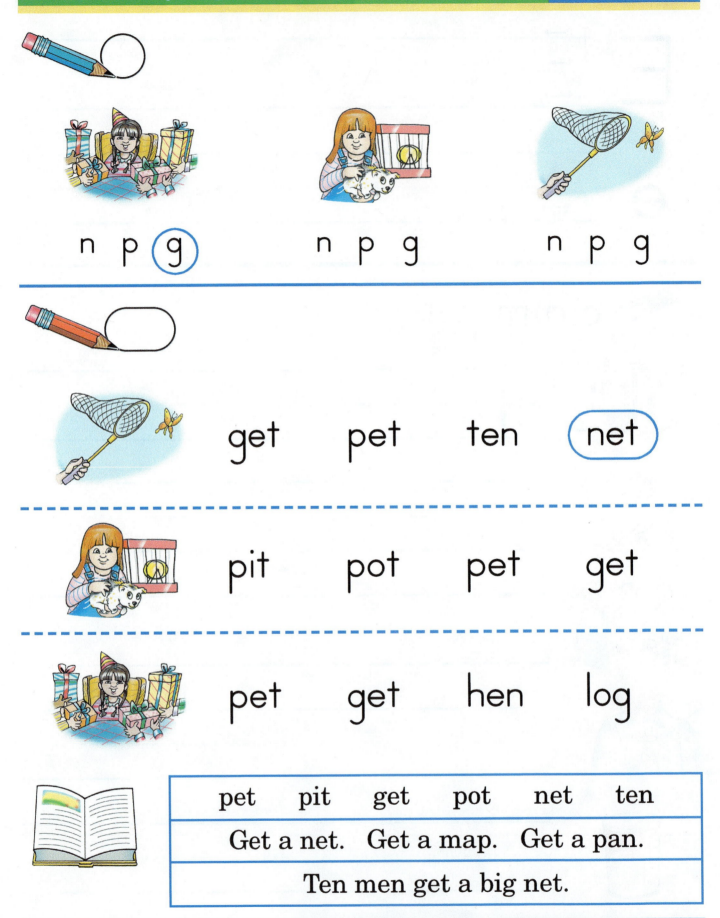

n p (g)   n p g   n p g

get   pet   ten   (net)

pit   pot   pet   get

pet   get   hen   log

pet	pit	get	pot	net	ten
Get a net.	Get a map.	Get a pan.			
Ten men get a big net.					

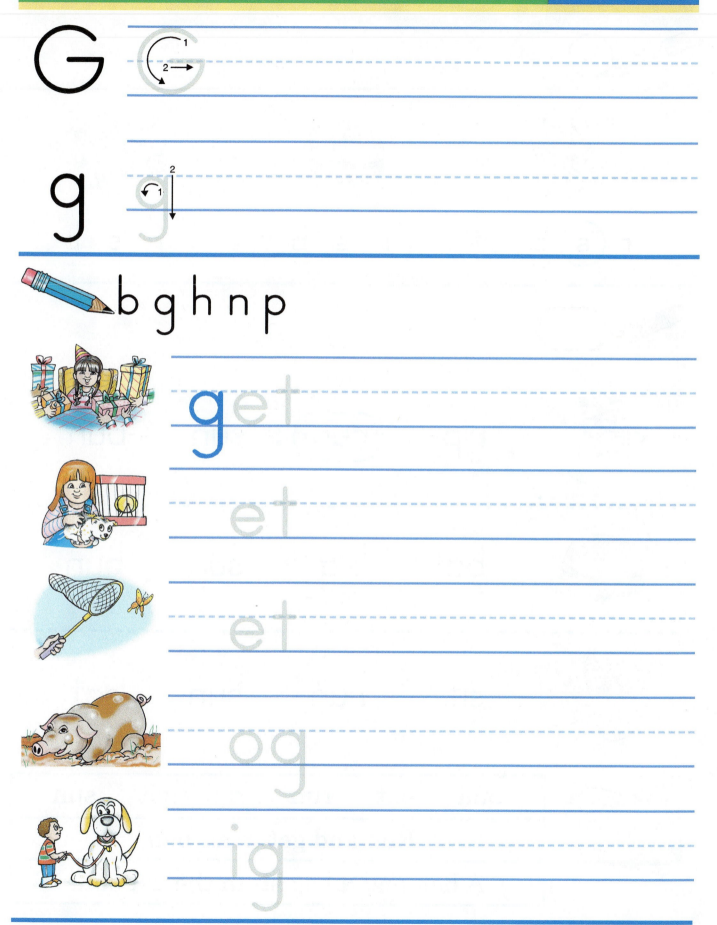

b g h n p

get

et

et

og

ig

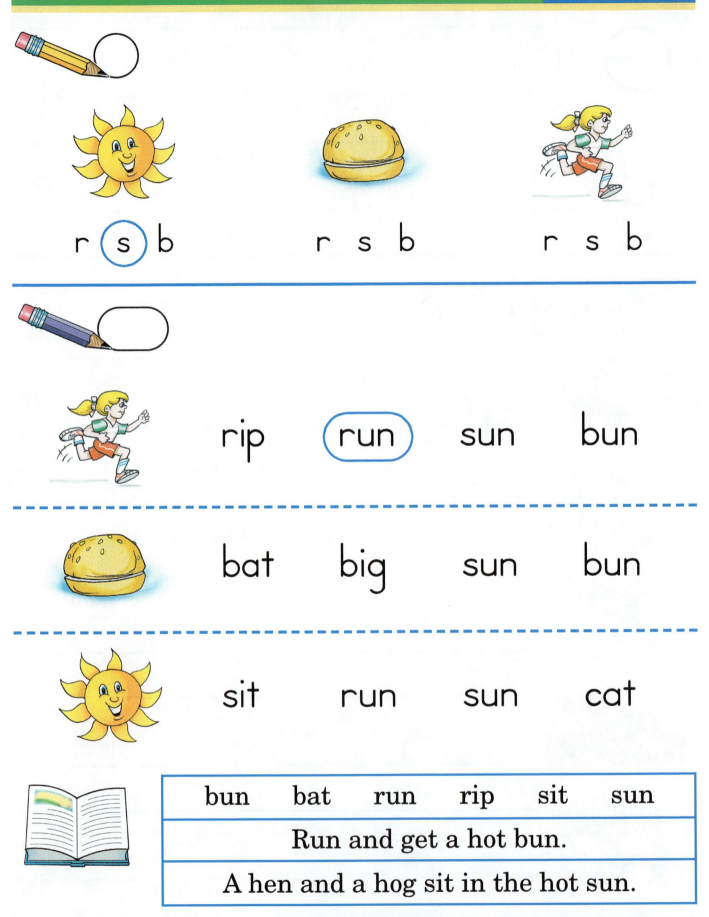

r (s) b   r s b   r s b

rip   (run)   sun   bun

bat   big   sun   bun

sit   run   sun   cat

| bun | bat | run | rip | sit | sun |

Run and get a hot bun.

A hen and a hog sit in the hot sun.

U

u

b g r s t

sun

un

un

et

en

m b j   m b j   m b j

big   bun   bug   jug

run   mat   men   mug

get   jug   bug   fog

bug   bun   mug   jug   big   bug

Get a big mug.   Get a big jug.

A big bug and a cat sit on a log in the sun.

J J

j j

b j m n s

mug

ug

ug

un

et

1.

2.

3.

4.

5.

6.

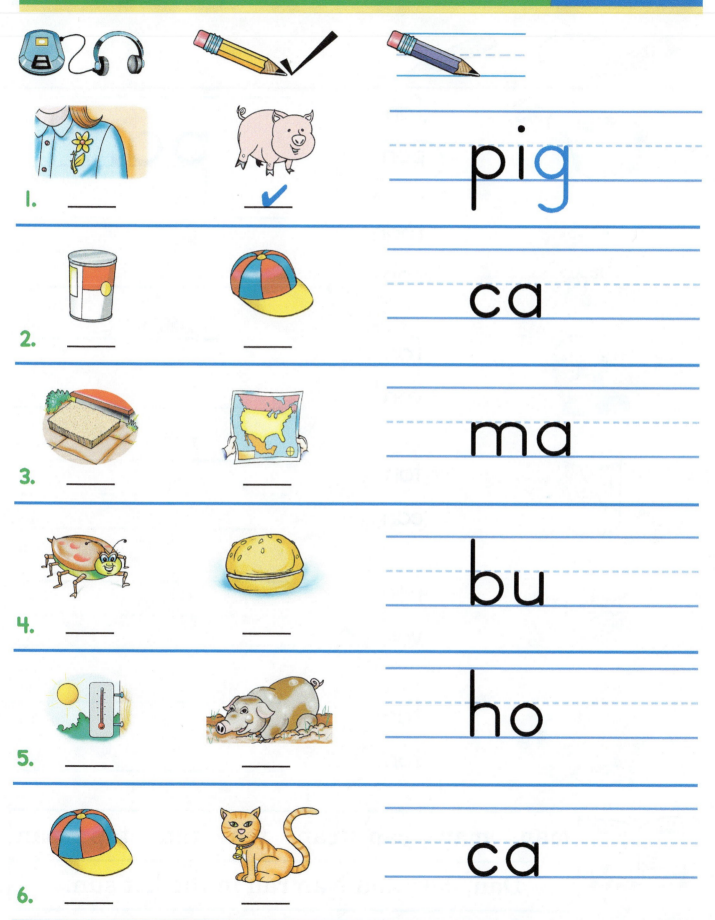

1. ____ ____ pig

2. ____ ____ ca

3. ____ ____ ma

4. ____ ____ bu

5. ____ ____ ho

6. ____ ____ ca

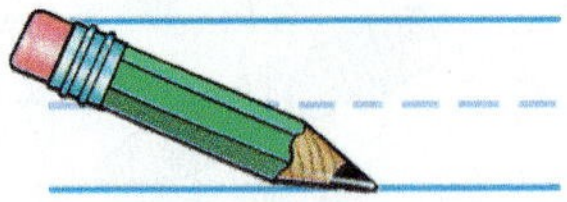

fan
(pan)

man
ran

fan
van

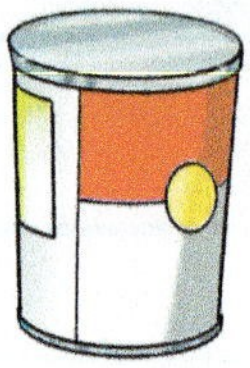

tan
can

ran
van

fan
tan

pan

man   map   can   cap   ten   tan   tap   pan

Dan, Jan, and Nan ran in the hot sun.

cap

gap

sap

rap

nap

map

lap

sap

tap

rap

gap

lap

cap

ran   rap   rip   cap   can   nap   pan   pin

Get a cap and a map.   Nap on the cot.

hat
(bat)

cat
sat

hat
fat

fat
vat

mat
rat

vat
mat

bat

cat   cap   can   map   man   mat   sat   sit

A fat cat and a fat rat sat on a big mat.

pad
dad

mad
sad

lad
mad

bad
pad

lad
dad

lad
bad

pad

| mad | mat | sad | sap | lap | lad | pad | pan |

A sad lad sat on a lap.   Dad sat on a hat.

1. _____ ✔ _____
2. _____ _____
3. _____ _____
4. _____ _____
5. _____ _____
6. _____ _____
7. _____ _____
8. _____ _____

rag
(wag)

wag

tag
rag

jam
yam

jam
ham

bag
dam

tag
dam

| bag | bad | bat | tag | tap | jam | rag | ran |

Get jam, ham, a yam, and a can in a big bag.

fig
(wig)

dig
fig

big
rig

pig
dig

jig
rig

fig
rig

wig

fig   fin   pig   pin   win   wig   big   bag

A pig, a rat, and a big cat dig and dig.

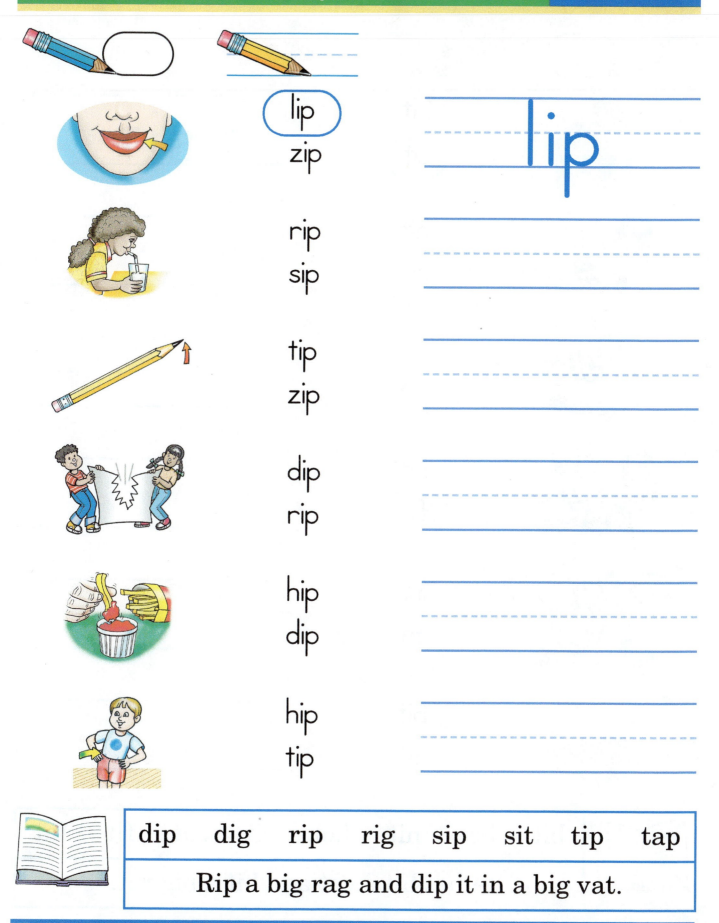

lip
zip

rip
sip

tip
zip

dip
rip

hip
dip

hip
tip

lip

dip   dig   rip   rig   sip   sit   tip   tap

Rip a big rag and dip it in a big vat.

zit

(sit)

hit

kit

lit

pit

bit

fit

lit

zit

bit

kit

sit

| bit | bat | hit | hot | sit | sat | fit | fat |

A bat hit a cat and bit a big rat.

hot
dot

got
pot

lot
tot

dot
cot

tot
lot

cot
pot

hot

got   get   hot   hat   pot   pit   cot   cat

A tot sat on a cot. Dad got a pot.

bog
(fog)

log
mop

hop
top

hog
pop

top
log

pop
bog

fog

bog   bag   big   tip   tap   top   mop   map

Hop on a log in a big bog.   Dad got a mop.

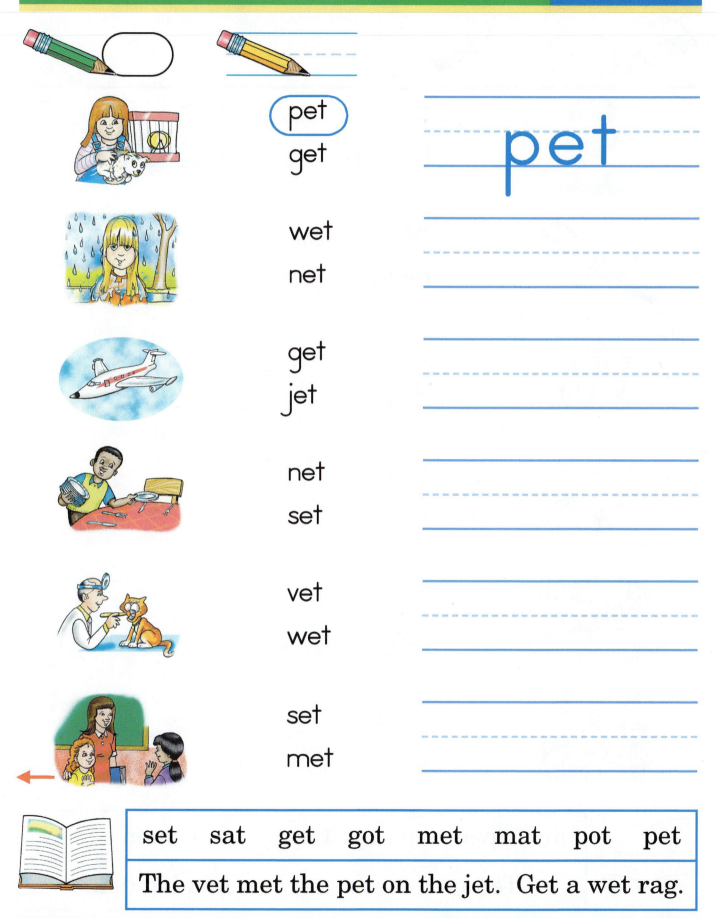

pet
get

wet
net

get
jet

net
set

vet
wet

set
met

pet

set sat get got met mat pot pet

The vet met the pet on the jet. Get a wet rag.

Ben

Pam

den

pen

ten

den

men

hen

den

ten

man

men

Ben

| pin | pen | pan | tan | ten | men | man |

Ten men met a wet hen in a big den.

bug
mug

tug
hug

rug
mug

tug
jug

dug
jug

dug
hug

bug

bug   bag   big   rag   rug   tug   dug   dig

A bug sat in a big jug.   A hog dug in a lot.

sun

(run)

fun
bun

nut
hut

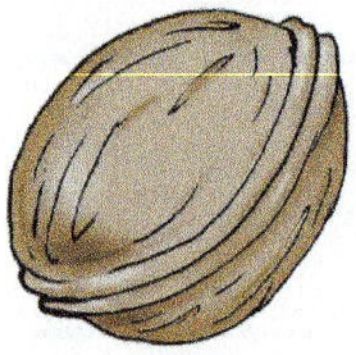

nut
cut

run
rut

cut
sun

run

fun   fan   hut   hit   cut   cot   nut   net

Get a hot bun and cut it in the hut.

tub
bud

sub
cup

rub
bud

cub
cup

rub
pup

sub
mud

tub

cub   cup   rub   rut   bud   bug   tug   tub

The cub and the pup dug and dug in the mud.

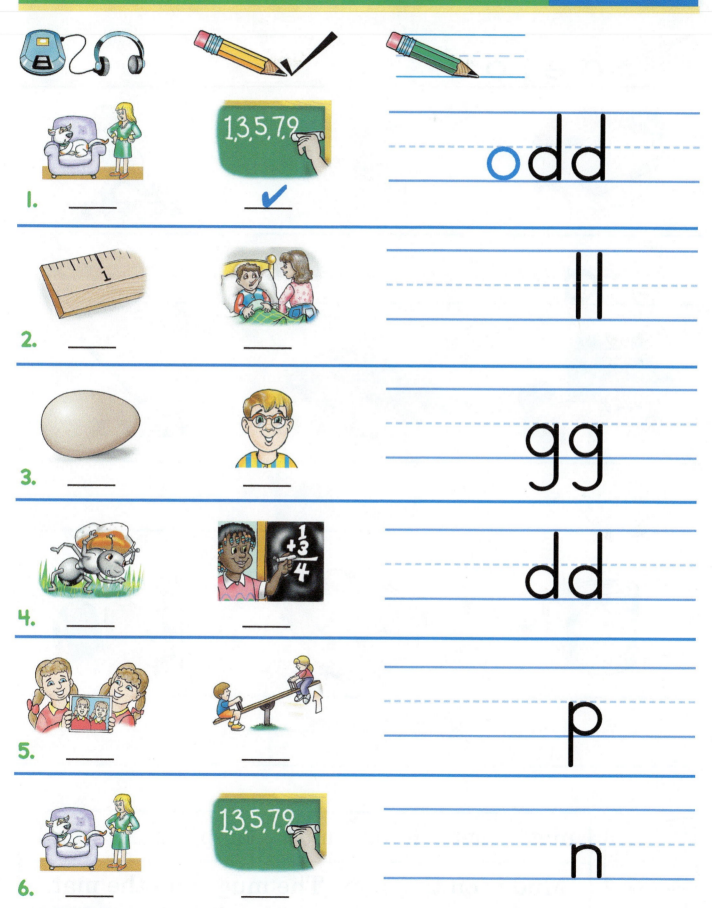

1. _____ _____ odd

2. _____ _____ ll

3. _____ _____ gg

4. _____ _____ dd

5. _____ _____ p

6. _____ _____ n

aeiou

m a t

m ___ m ___ m

m ___ d

m ___ t

m ___ ll

m ___ p

m ___ g

m ___ tt

m ___ n

mat   met   man   mop   map   mug   mill

Mud is on the mop.   The mug is on the mat.

aeiou

n e t

n __ t

n __ p

n __ d

n __ t

n __ t

n __ ck

N __ ck

N __ t

nod   not   nut   nit   net   Nat   nap

The nit is not on the neck. Nat and Nick nod.

1.

2.

3.

4.

5.

6.

mud

a e i o u

f i n

f g

f n

f d

f g

f n

f

f ll

f t

fat   fan   fun   fin   fig   fog   fed   fell

Nat fed the fat pig a big fig and a nut.

a e i o u

s **a** t   s n   s p

s b   s t   s d

s b   s ll   s ck

sit   set   sat   sad   sock   sob   sub   sun

Sit in the sub. Sit in the sun. Sell the sock.

set

1.

2.

3.

4.

5.

6.

hem   h t   h g

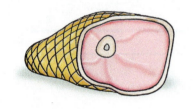

h m   h n   h p

h t   h g   h p

hut   hit   hat   hot   hip   hop   hem   ham

The hog and the hen hop on a hat in the hut.

a e i o u

j u g

j _ t

j _ m

j _ b

j _ g

j _ g

J _ ff

J _ ll

J _ ck

jig   jug   jog   job   Jack   jam   jet

Jeff and Jill sell jam and a jug to Jack.

1. ✔ ____   ____   hit

2. ____   ____

3. ____   ____

4. ____   ____

5. ____   ____

6. ____   ____

a e i o u

r u g   r _ t   r _ p

r _   r _ d   r _ n

r _ g   r _ n   r _ c k

rat   ran   run   rug   rig   rip   red   rod

The red rod is on the rock.   The rat ran on the rug.

a e i o u

o g   p   g

p   d   t

t   d   ck

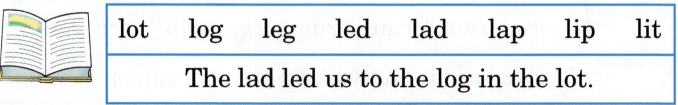

lot   log   leg   led   lad   lap   lip   lit

The lad led us to the log in the lot.

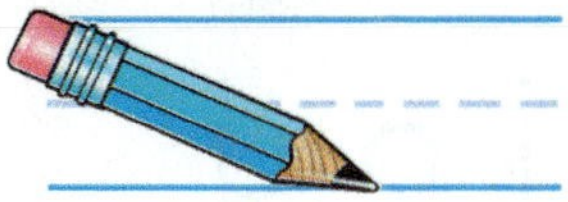

1. ✔ ___   ___   log

2. ___   ___

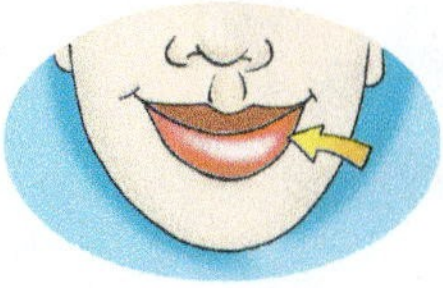

3. ___   ___

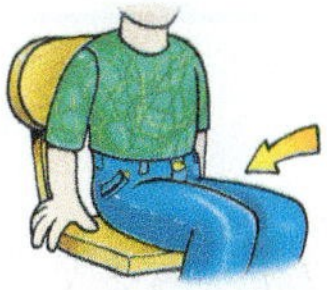

4. ___   ___

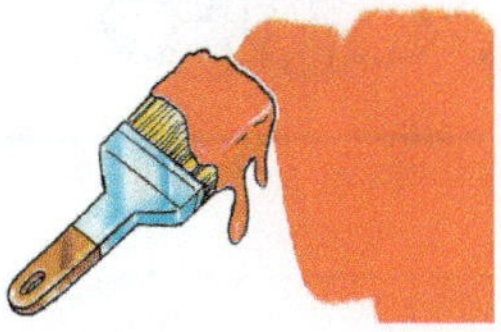

5. ___   ___

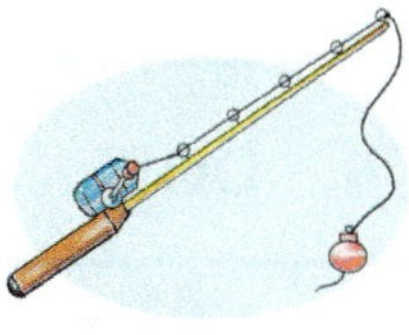

6. ___   ___

a e i o u

b a g

b _ s

b _ d

b _ b

b _ g

b _ t

b _ g

b _ g

b _ g

bus   bug   bag   big   beg   bog   Bob   bib

Bob is on the bus with a big bag.

a e i o u

p e n

p _ d

p _ p

p _ p

p _ n

p _ t

p _ p

p _ g

p _ t

pen   pin   pan   pad   pup   pop   pot   pet

The pup and the pig sat with a pad and a pen.

1. pet

2.

3.

4.

5.

6.

a e i o u

dig   d m   d n

d p   d t   d ck

d g   d d   d ll

dig   dip   dot   dad   duck   dug   den

Dad is in the den with the duck.

a e i o u

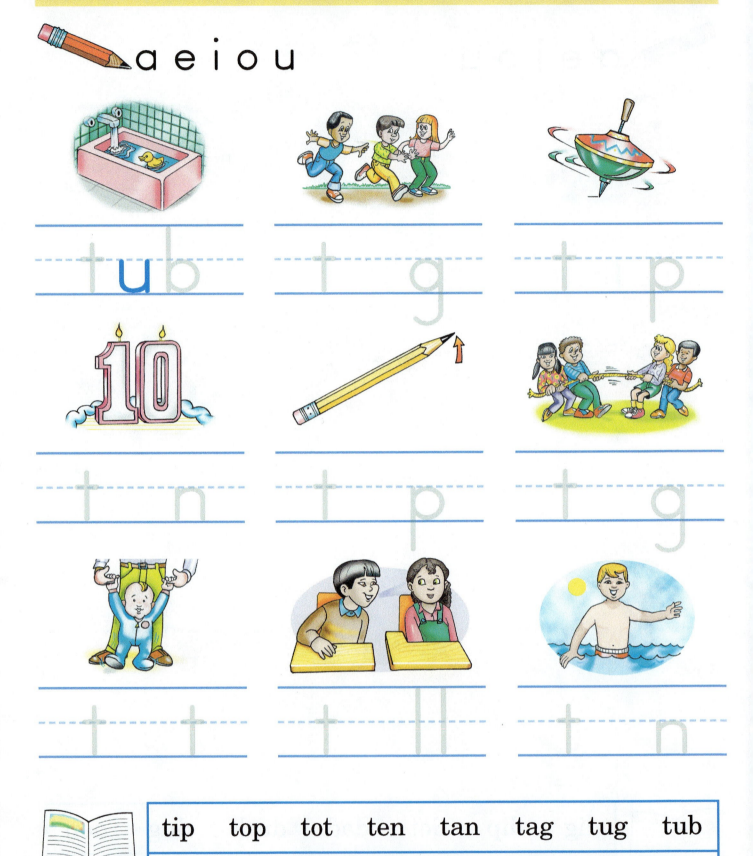

t u b

t   g

t   p

t   n

t   p

t   g

t

t l l

t   n

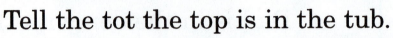

tip   top   tot   ten   tan   tag   tug   tub

Tell the tot the top is in the tub.

1. tag

73

g e t   g _ m   g _ s

g ll   g _ t   g _ p

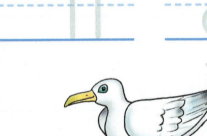

g ll   g _ t

| get | got | gas | gull | gill | gap | gum |

Bob got gum and Jill got gas. The gull got a bug.

a e i o u

c **u** t   k _ d   c _ d

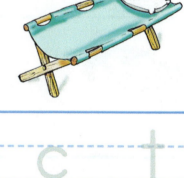

c _ t   c _ b   c _ t

k _ t   c _ n   K _ n

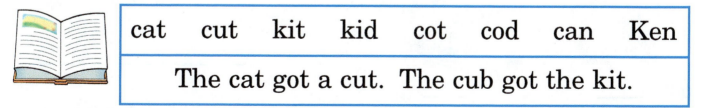

cat   cut   kit   kid   cot   cod   can   Ken

The cat got a cut. The cub got the kit.

1.

2.

3.

4.

5.

6.

DICTIONARY
pages 52–55

(t)
p

t
(p)

t
(p)

(t)
p

t
n

t
n

t
n

t
n

s
b

s
b

s
b

s
b

p
n

p
n

p
n

p
n

m
g

m
g

m
g

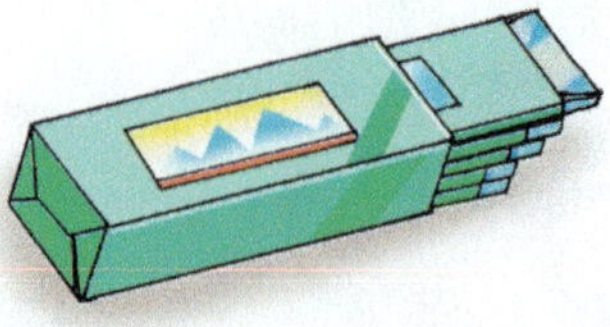

m
g

t
p

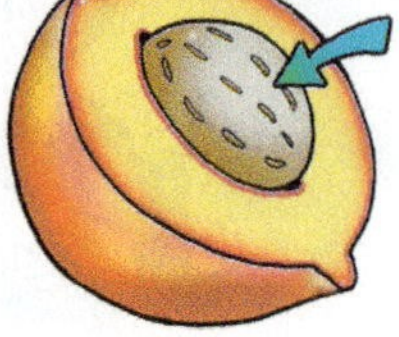

t
p

t
p

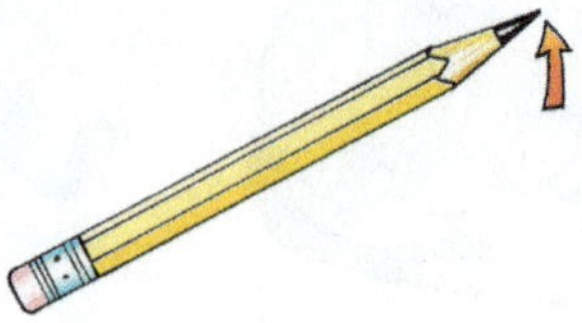

t
p

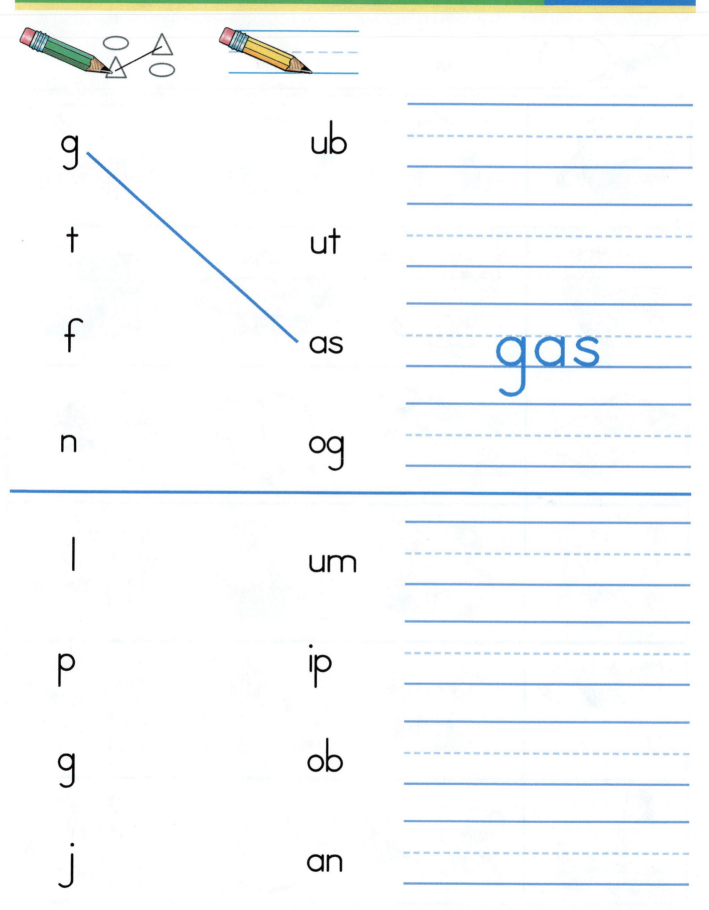

g

t

f

n

l

p

g

j

ub

ut

as

og

um

ip

ob

an

gas

RHYMING WORDS REVIEW

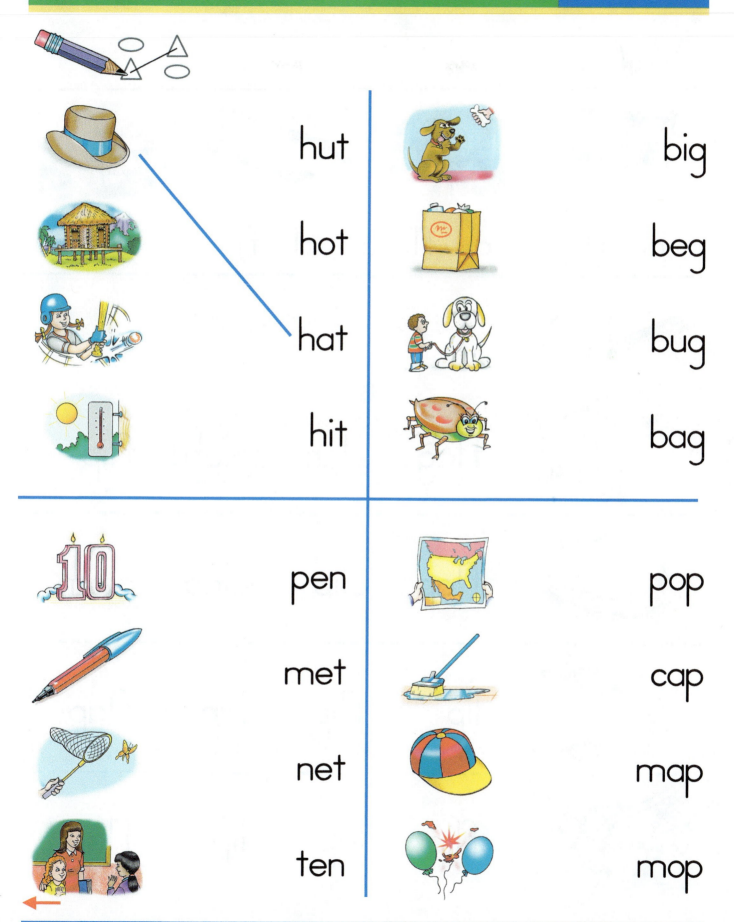

hut

hot

hat

hit

big

beg

bug

bag

pen

met

net

ten

pop

cap

map

mop

cl （fl）   cl fl   cl fl   cl fl

flag   clap   (club)   flip

flap   clip   clap   clam

lip   flip   lap   flap

flip   lap   lip   flap

cl fl

flag

ub

ip

ip

ap

at

am

ap

lip   clip   lap   clap   cub   club   fat   flat

The flag is flat. The cub can clap.

(dr) tr   tr fr   dr cr   dr fr

crop (crab) trap frog

fan ran frog Fran

trap tot trot drop

trap flag drum crop

cr dr fr Fr tr

drum

og

ab

ap

op

op

ot

an

fog   frog   tap   rap   trap   fan   ran   Fran

The crab and the frog drop the drum.

INITIAL CONSONANT BLENDS *sk, sl, sm*

sk (sl)　　sm sk　　sl sk　　sm sl

　　slip　　smog sell　　(smell)

　　slip　　sip　　skip　　skin

　　led　　sled　　slug　　skip

　　sip　　lip　　skip　　slip

sk   sl   sm

s|ed

ip

og

ug

ell

in

ip

ot

sip   lip   slip   skip   lot   slot   led   sled

Skip in the lot. Slip on the sled.

sp ⬭st⬭   st   sw   st   sp   sw   st

⬭stick⬭   stem   step   stop

stop   spot   pin   spin

step   top   stop   spot

stop   top   spot   pot

sp st sw

stem

__in

__im

__ap

__ep

__ot

__op

__ick

pin   spin   pot   spot   top   stop   tick   stick

Spin the top. Step on the stick. Stop and swim.

1. _____ ✔

2. _____ _____

3. _____ _____

4. _____ _____

5. _____ _____

6. _____ _____

7. _____ _____

8. _____ _____

9. _____ _____

10. _____ _____

DICTIONARY
pages 64–67

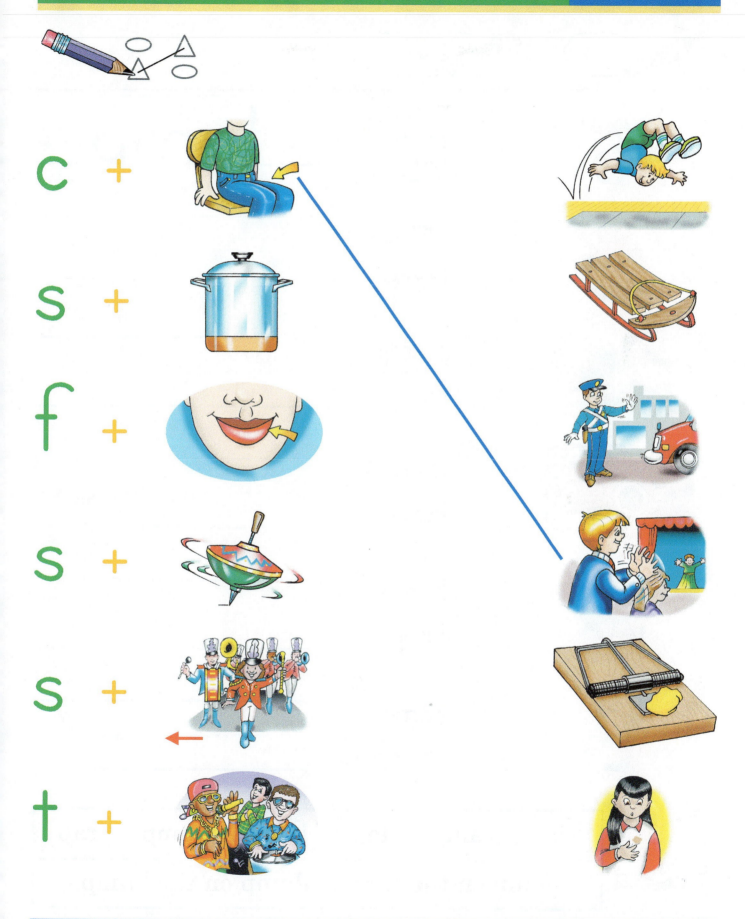

ramp
(lamp)

jump
bump

stamp
camp

dump
bump

hump
jump

ramp
stamp

lamp

cap   camp   lap   lamp   ramp   rap

Jump on the ramp.   Jump on the bump.

hand (circled) / sand		hand
mend / wind		
pond / stand		
band / bend		
band / bend		
sand / stand		

win   wind   men   mend   sad   sand   bad   band

The band can stand in the sand at the pond.

hunt
(ant)

went
tent

dent
bent

print
plant

tent
dent

print
hunt

ant

ten   tent   den   dent   wet   went   hut   hunt

The ant went on the wet plant in the tent.

lk   lt   ft

left   mi___   be___

___e   gi___   me___

li___   ra___

rat   raft   met   melt   lit   lift   left

Lift the gift. The milk is on the left.

fast

vest

rest

nest

test

west

last

best

vest

rest

west

best

fast

net   nest   fat   fast   west   wet   vet   vest

Run fast, run best, run west, and rest.

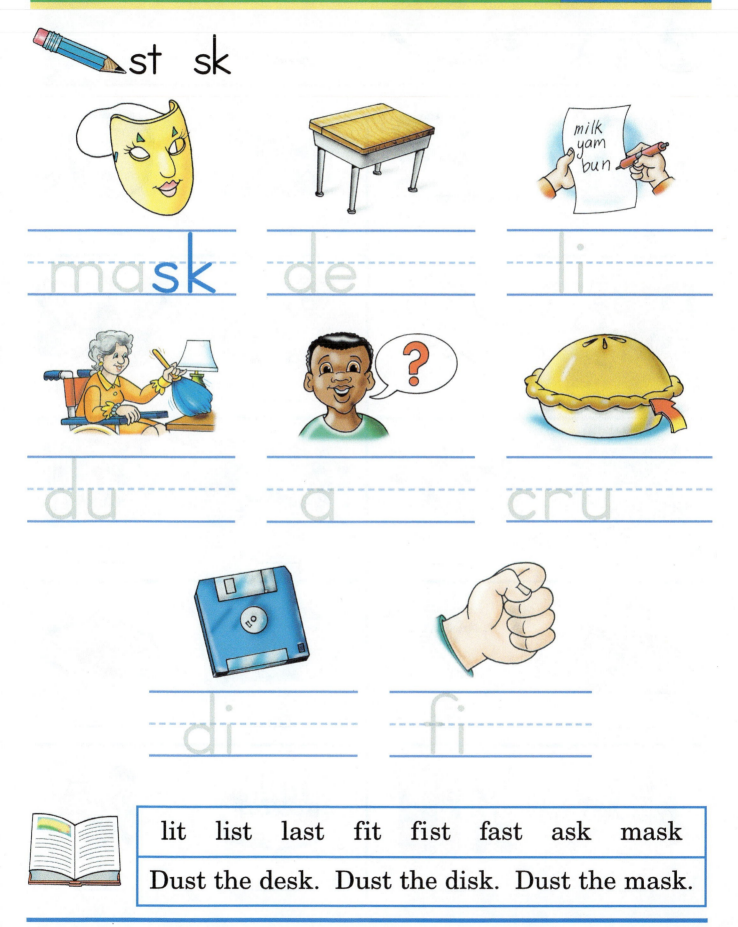

st sk

ma**sk**   de___   li___

du___   a___   cru___

di___   fi___

lit   list   last   fit   fist   fast   ask   mask

Dust the desk. Dust the disk. Dust the mask.

1. _____ ✔

2. _____ _____

3. _____ _____

4. _____ _____

5. _____ _____

6. _____ _____

7. _____ _____

8. _____ _____

9. _____ _____

10. _____ _____

– d

– t

– m

– s

– f

– s

box fix fox mix six wax

fix

six sock fix fig bog box wax wag

The fox and the frog fix the box on the desk.

ss ff

glass dre cli

ki hu cla

pre gra

class glass grass press kiss fix cliff

The dress is in the box in the class.

ill
hill

sell
fell

shell
smell

gull
gill

spill
spell

well
mill

fill   fell   spill   spell   sell   shell   smell

The bell fell in the well at the mill on the hill.

Bill   Fill   Smell   Spell   Spill   Tell   Yell

Fill the glass.

_____ Jill.

_____ at the gull.

_____ is ill.

_____ the milk.

_____ cat.

_____ it.

lock
(clock)

clock

black
block

track
trick

sick
sock

black
back

kick
pick

lock   block   clock   sick   stick   back   black

Kick the black rock. Rick is sick.

| brick | duck | rock | sick | sock | trick | truck |

The ___**sock**___ is black.

Sit on the _____.

Rick is _____.

The _____ is big.

The _____ is red.

Jack did a _____.

The _____ is in the pond.

quack quick quill quilt quit quiz

quiz

quiz quit kit quick kick crab quack

The quill is on the quilt. The duck can quack.

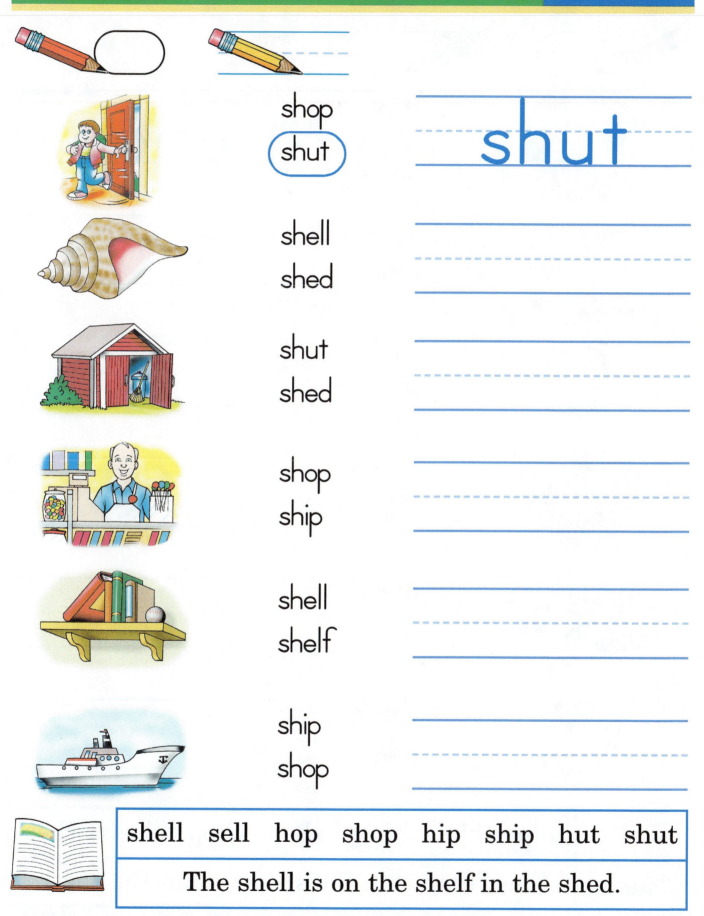

shop
(shut)

shell
shed

shut
shed

shop
ship

shell
shelf

ship
shop

shut

shell   sell   hop   shop   hip   ship   hut   shut

The shell is on the shelf in the shed.

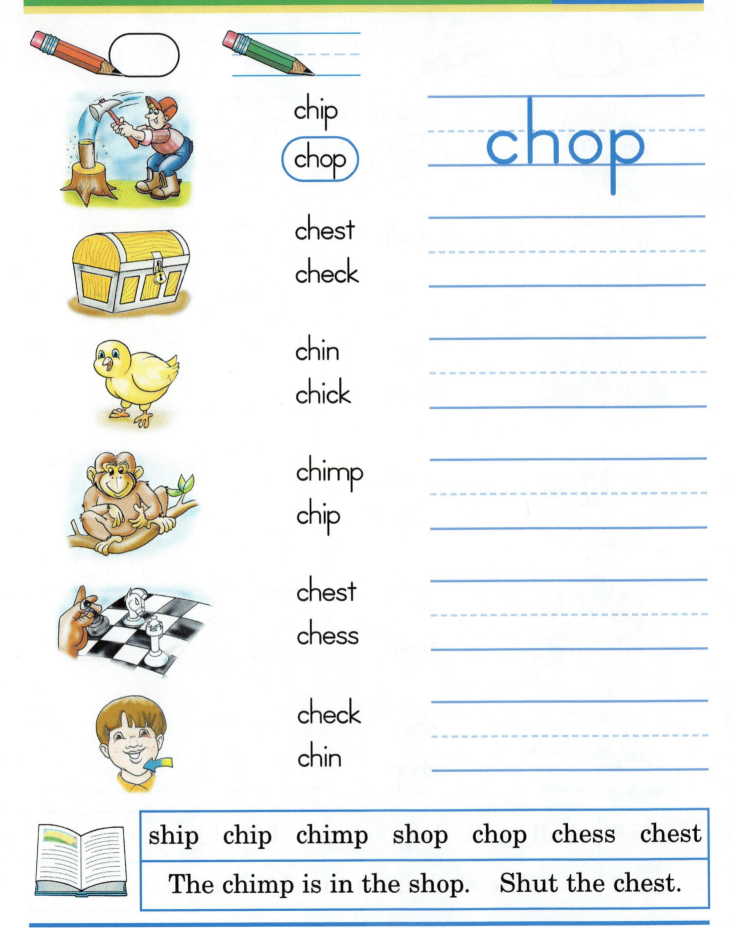

chip
(chop)

chest
check

chin
chick

chimp
chip

chest
chess

check
chin

chop

ship   chip   chimp   shop   chop   chess   chest

The chimp is in the shop.   Shut the chest.

th wh

thick   in   en

ink   ich   at

ank   is

tick   thick   think   hat   that   hen   when

I think that hat is thick.   This chip is thin.

brush
trash

dish
fish

rash
mash

crash
trash

wish
fish

rash
dish

brush

rash   trash   crash   dish   disk   mash   mask

That brush is in the trash in the shed.

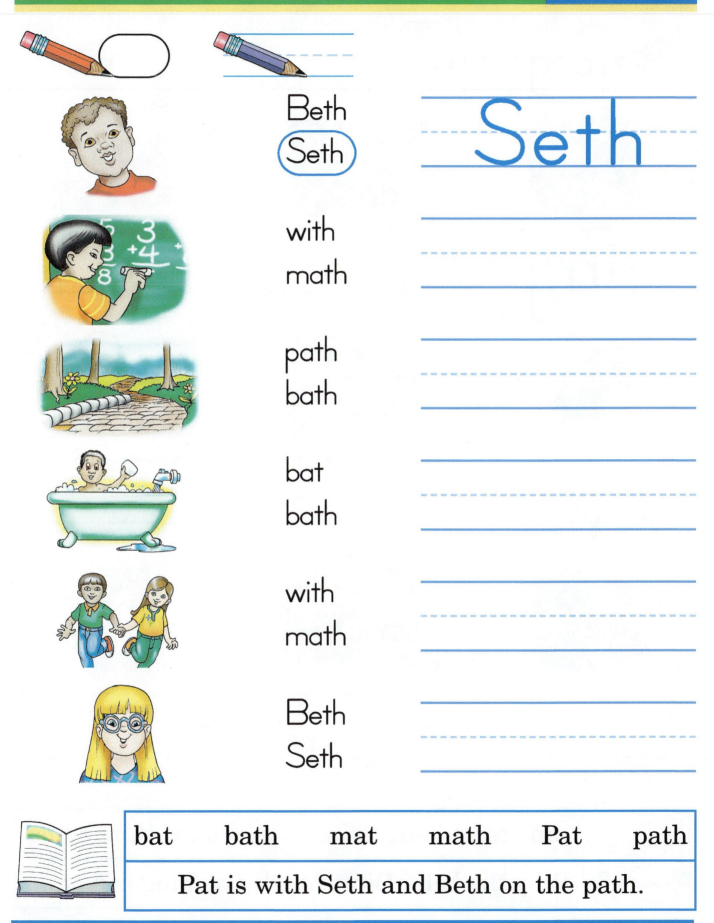

Beth
(Seth)

Seth

with
math

path
bath

bat
bath

with
math

Beth
Seth

| bat | bath | mat | math | Pat | path |

Pat is with Seth and Beth on the path.

FINAL CONSONANT DIGRAPH *ng*

DICTIONARY
pages 86–87

ang ing

king   s   h

sw   f   sl

b   s   r

ran rang win wing fan fang thin thing

Ring the bell. Ding dong! The king can sing.

1. _____   _____   bring

2. _____   _____

3. _____   _____

4. _____   _____

5. _____   _____

6. _____   _____

ank ink unk

p**ink**

j

b

b

dr

tr

th

w

sk

pin pink tan tank bun bunk thin think

I think the sink is pink. The skunk can stink.

1.

2.

3.

4.

5.

6.

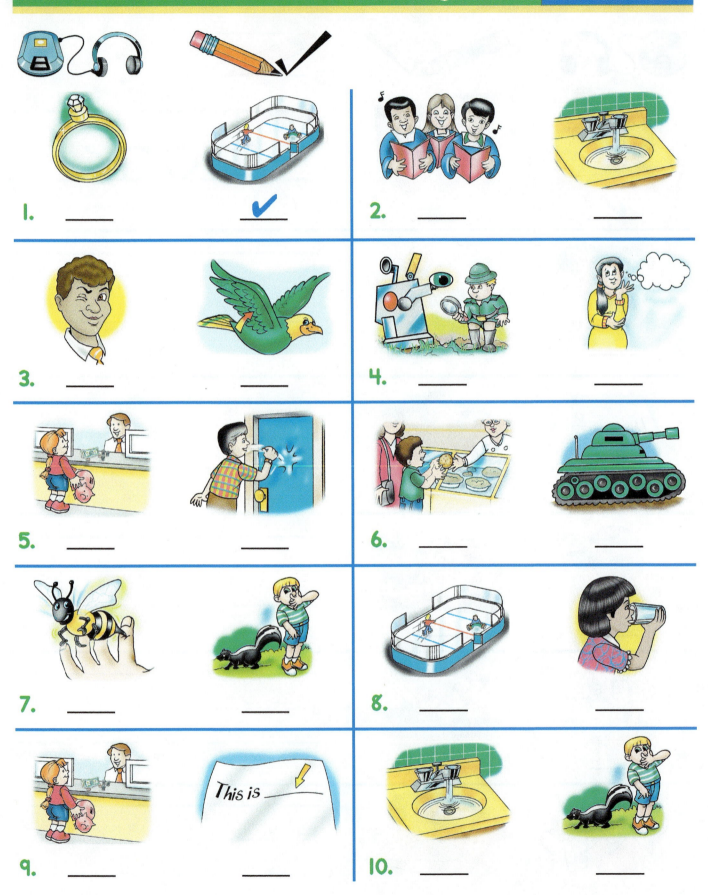

1. _____ ✔

2. _____ _____

3. _____ _____

4. _____ _____

5. _____ _____

6. _____ _____

7. _____ _____

8. _____ _____

9. _____ _____

10. _____ _____

This is _____

DICTIONARY
page 90

bench
lunch

which
rich

inch
pinch

which
lunch

branch
ranch

branch
ranch

bench

ran   ranch   pin   pinch   inch   rich   which

Sit on the bench.   Sit on the branch.

itch
(pitch)

pitch

catch
patch

Dutch
ditch

switch
sketch

pitch
patch

catch
sketch

cat   catch   pit   pitch   itch   Pat   patch

Catch the cat in the ditch.

m		(m)	(b)	b
r		r	x	x
ck		ck	ch	ch
s		s	d	d
ch		ch	th	th
sh		sh	th	th

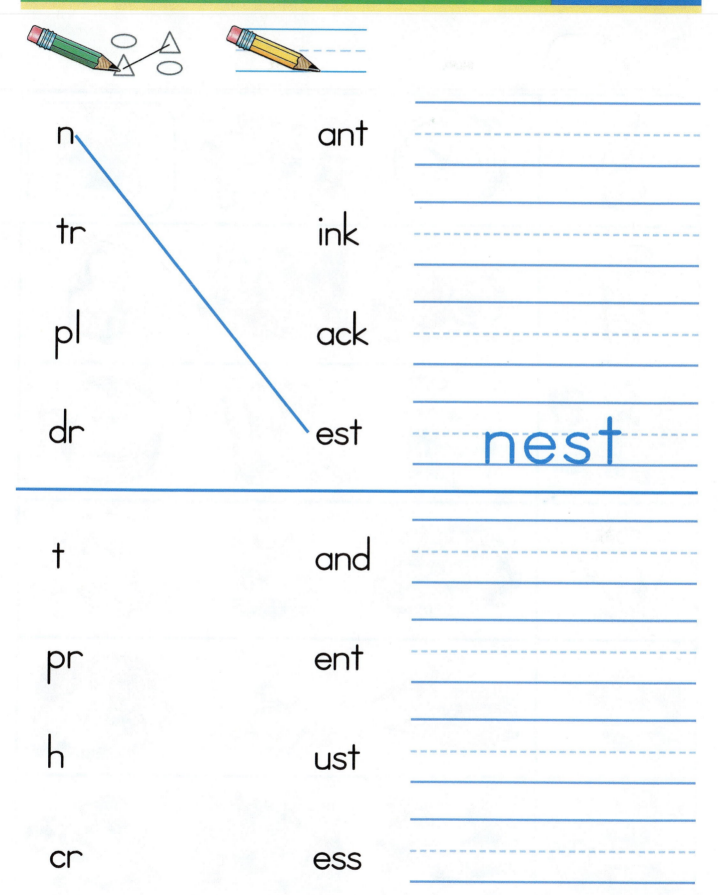

n   ant

tr   ink

pl   ack

dr   est

nest

t   and

pr   ent

h   ust

cr   ess

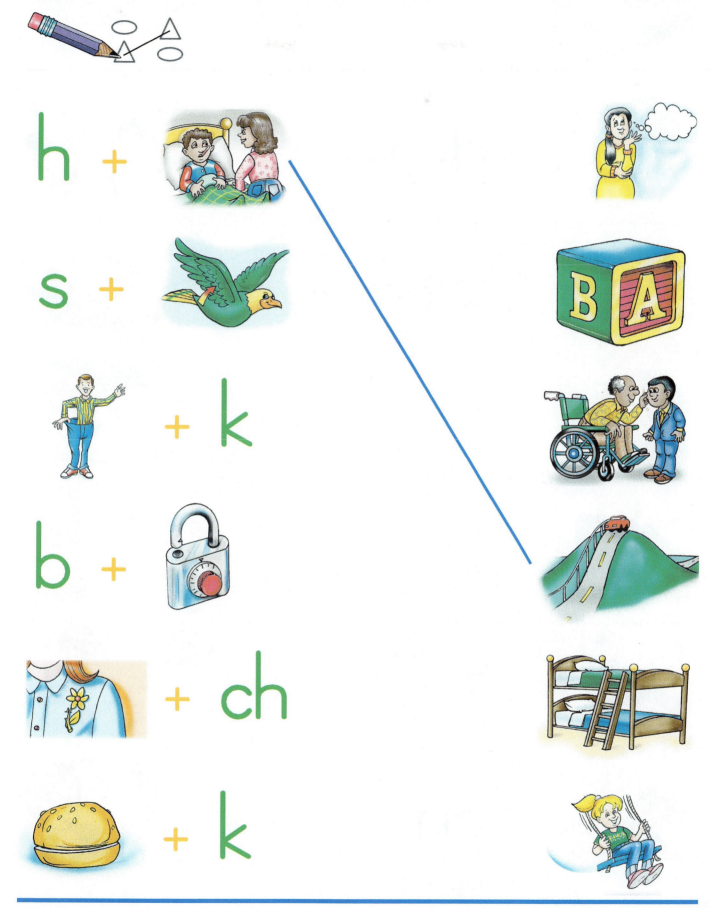

– d

– c

– s

– l

– t

– ch

DICTIONARY pages 106–107

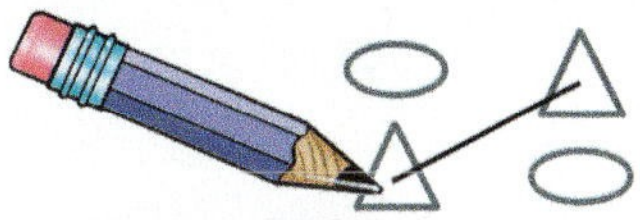

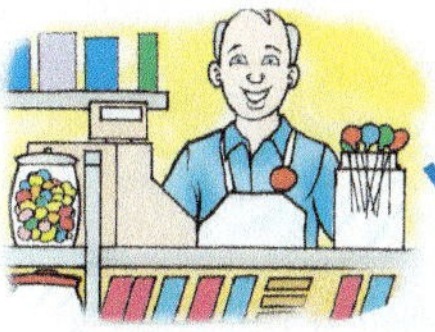

chop

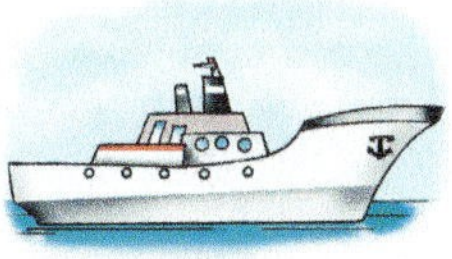

chip

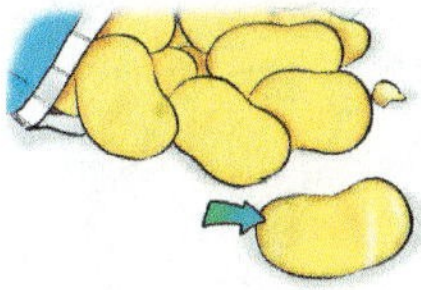

shop

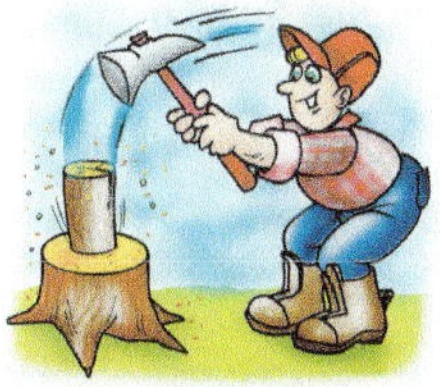

ship

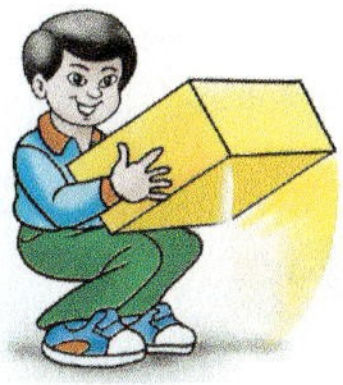

left

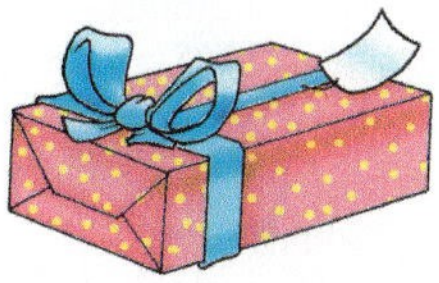

gift

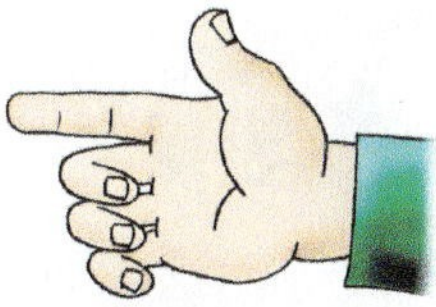

raft

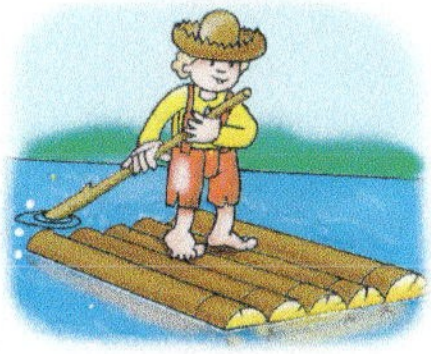

lift

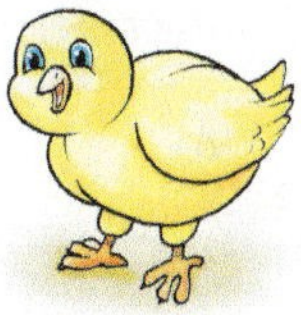

kick

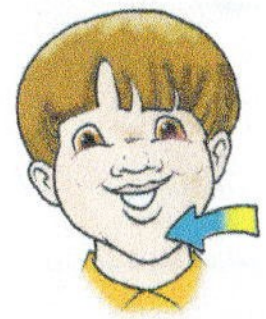

chick

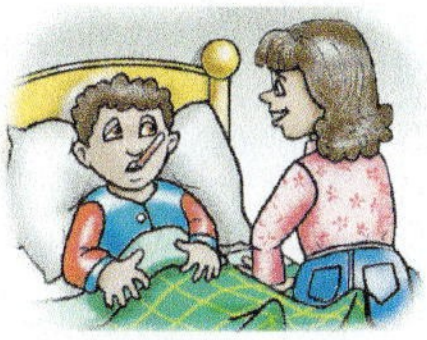

sick

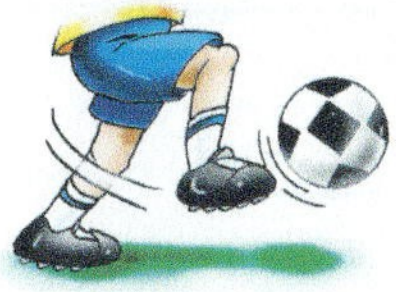

chin

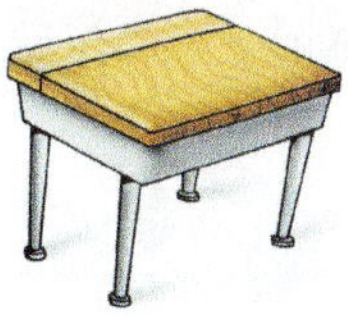

dish

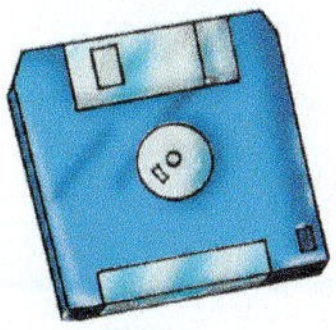

disk

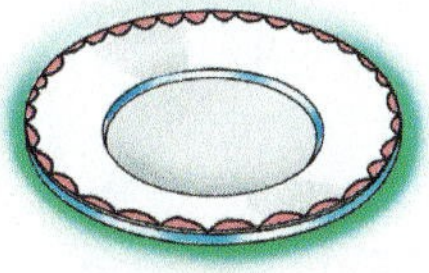

fish

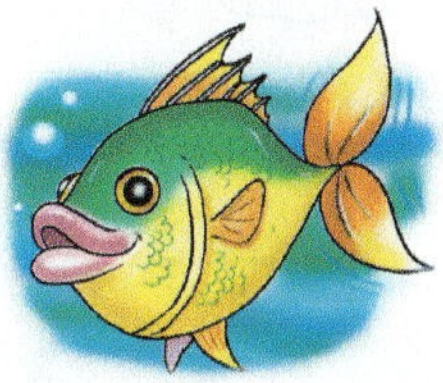

desk

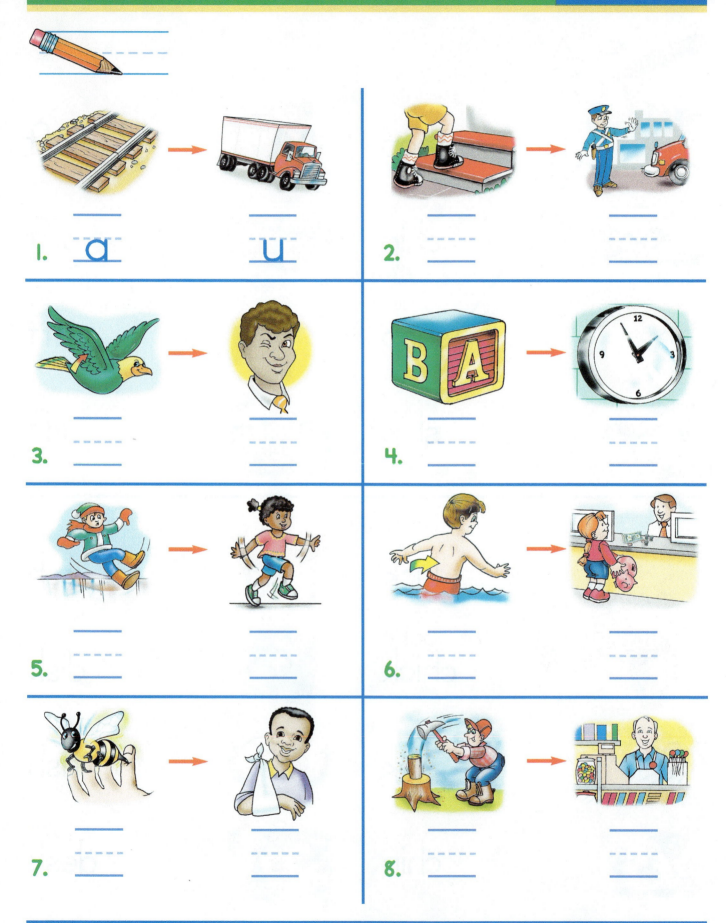

1. a → u

2.

3.

4.

5.

6.

7.

8.

rake
cake

gate
game

mane
name

plate
plane

save
bake

ate
gave

cake

can cane man mane tap tape cap cape

The rake is at the gate. I ate the cake on the plate.

cake   name   save   skate   snake   tape

1. take — snake

2. grape

3. late

4. wave

5. wake

6. same

DICTIONARY
pages 112–113

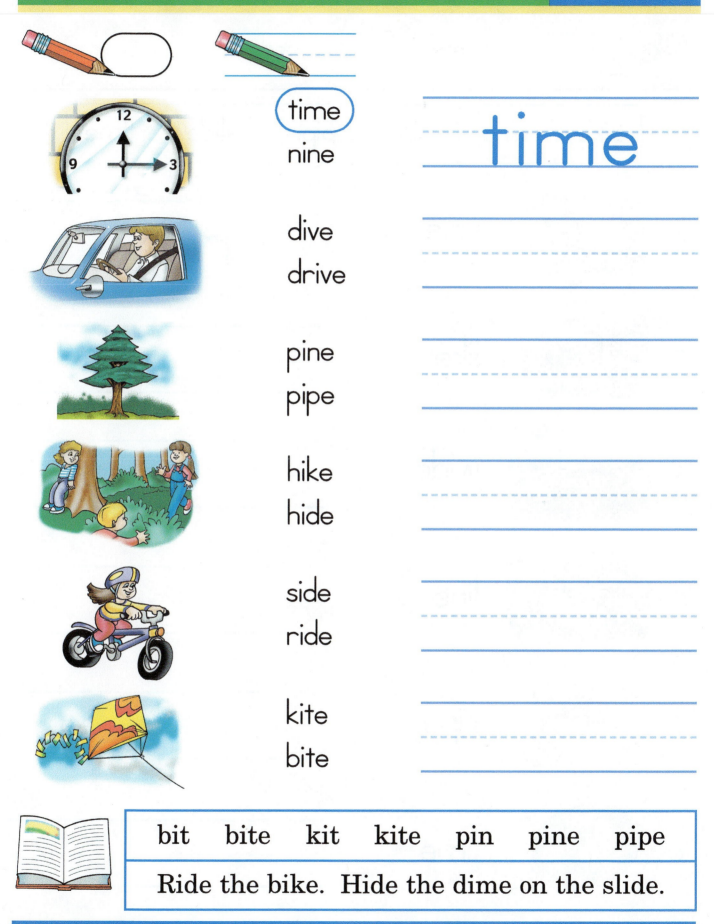

time
nine

dive
drive

pine
pipe

hike
hide

side
ride

kite
bite

time

bit   bite   kit   kite   pin   pine   pipe

Ride the bike. Hide the dime on the slide.

| bike | nine | pine | pipe | slide | time |

1. vine   nine

2. like

3. wide

4. line

5. ripe

6. lime

note
home

cone
bone

pole
hole

stove
stole

rode
robe

drove
rode

home

hole   home   dome   robe   rode   not   note

The mole stole a bone in a hole and rode home.

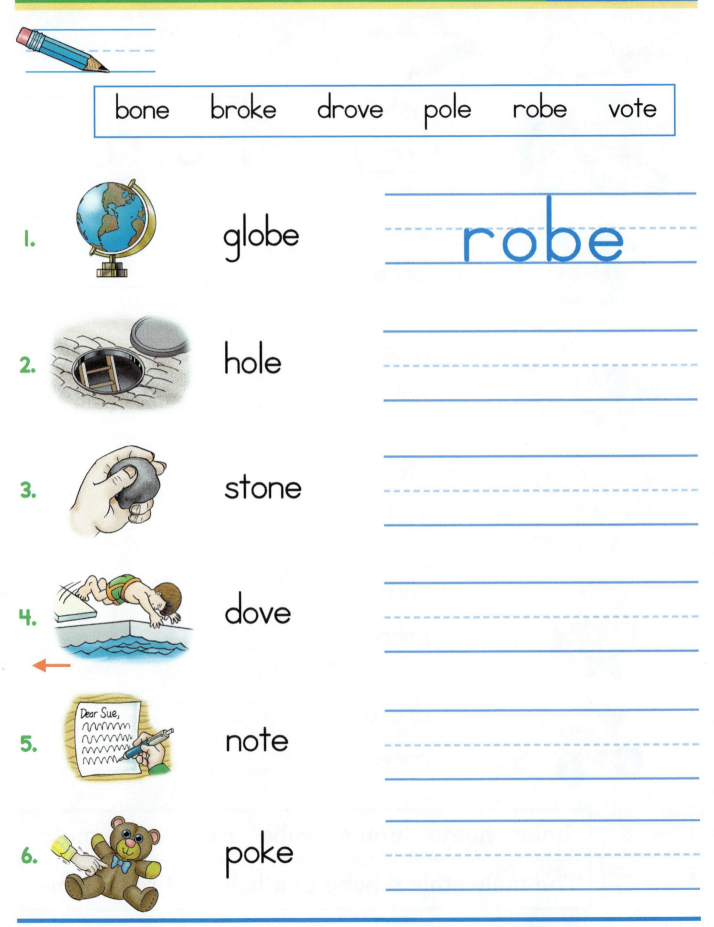

bone   broke   drove   pole   robe   vote

1. globe   robe

2. hole

3. stone

4. dove

5. note

6. poke

(cube)
tube

dune
duke

prune
flute

dune
tune

rule
rude

tube
cute

cube

| cub | cube | tub | tube | cut | cute | flute |

Luke is on a cute mule on a dune in June.

a i o u

gl o be   b __ ke   b __ ke

c __ ne   c __ ne   fl __ te

d __ me   sk __ te   m __ le

m __ le   k __ te   r __ le

 + e

 + e

 + e

+ e 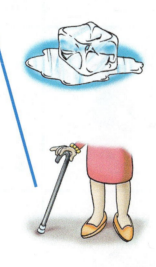 cane

+ e

+ e

DICTIONARY
pages 118–119

1. _____ ✔

2. _____ _____

3. _____ _____

4. _____ _____

5. _____ _____

6. _____ _____

7. _____ _____

8. _____ _____

9. _____ _____

10. _____ _____

bee
peel

feed
feet

see
seed

three
tree

sweep
sleep

green
queen

bee

sleep   sweep   sheep   see   tree   three   green

I see a bee in the green tree.   Feed the three sheep.

bee   feed   feet   meet   queen   sweep

1. beet — feet

2. deep

3. teen

4. weed

5. free

6. sheet

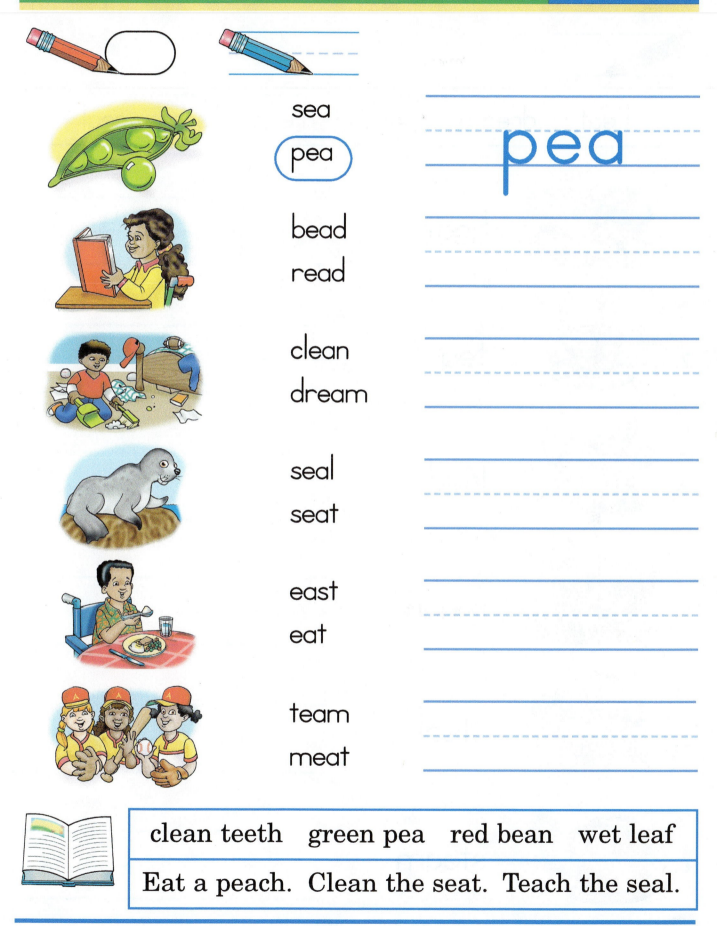

sea

(pea)

bead
read

clean
dream

seal
seat

east
eat

team
meat

pea

clean teeth   green pea   red bean   wet leaf

Eat a peach. Clean the seat. Teach the seal.

beat   dream   peach   read   sea   seal

1. heat   beat

2. tea

3. lead

4. mean

5. steal

6. steam

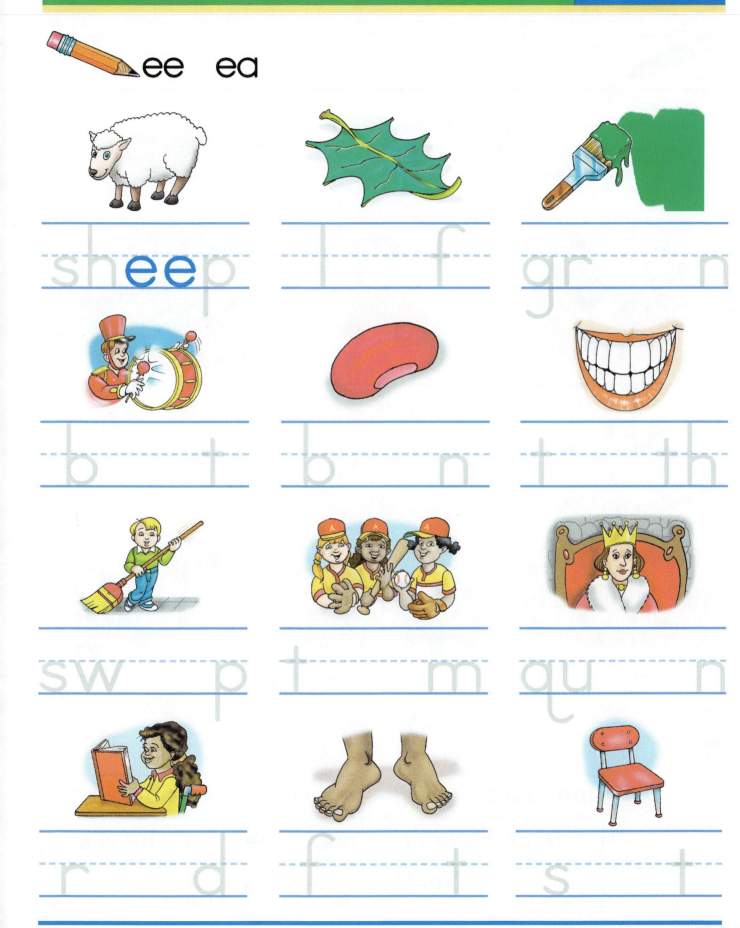

ee   ea

sh**ee**p

l___f

gr___n

b___t

b___n

t___th

sw___p

t___m

qu___n

r___d

f___t

s___t

go   he   me   no   she   we

she

me meet met she shed no note not

He and she meet me.   We go in the sea.

No, this is not a yo-yo.

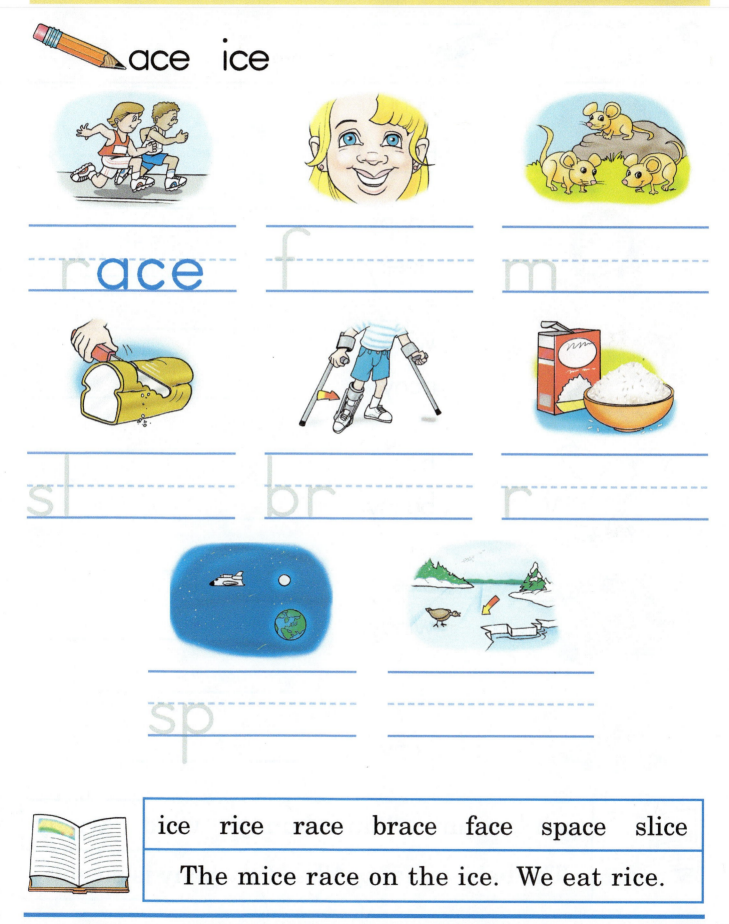

ace ice

r**ace**

f____

m____

s____

br____

r____

sp____

____

____

ice rice race brace face space slice

The mice race on the ice. We eat rice.

bunny
(penny)

happy
sleepy

windy
pony

bun
bunny

sleepy
windy

tiny
pony

penny

pen   penny   bun   bunny   wind   windy

The baby is happy. The tiny pony is sleepy.

sky

sky
dry

my
why

fry
cry

fry
fly

dry
fly

why
fry

| my pony | tiny fly | windy sky | baby cry |

Why did my tiny pony cry? Fly in the sky.

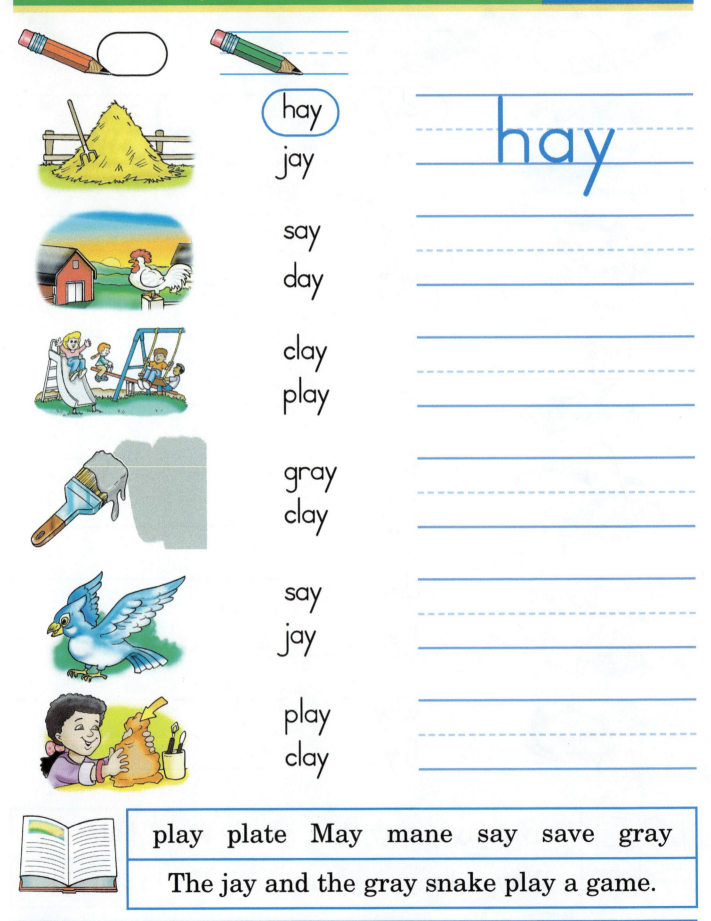

hay
jay

say
day

clay
play

gray
clay

say
jay

play
clay

hay

play plate May mane say save gray

The jay and the gray snake play a game.

chair paint rain sail tail train

He can __paint__.

The _____ is on the track.

The _____ is red.

I stand in the _____.

The cat has a cute _____.

She can _____ with the wind.

paint pail rain train sail chain chair

The gray paint is in the pail on the chair.

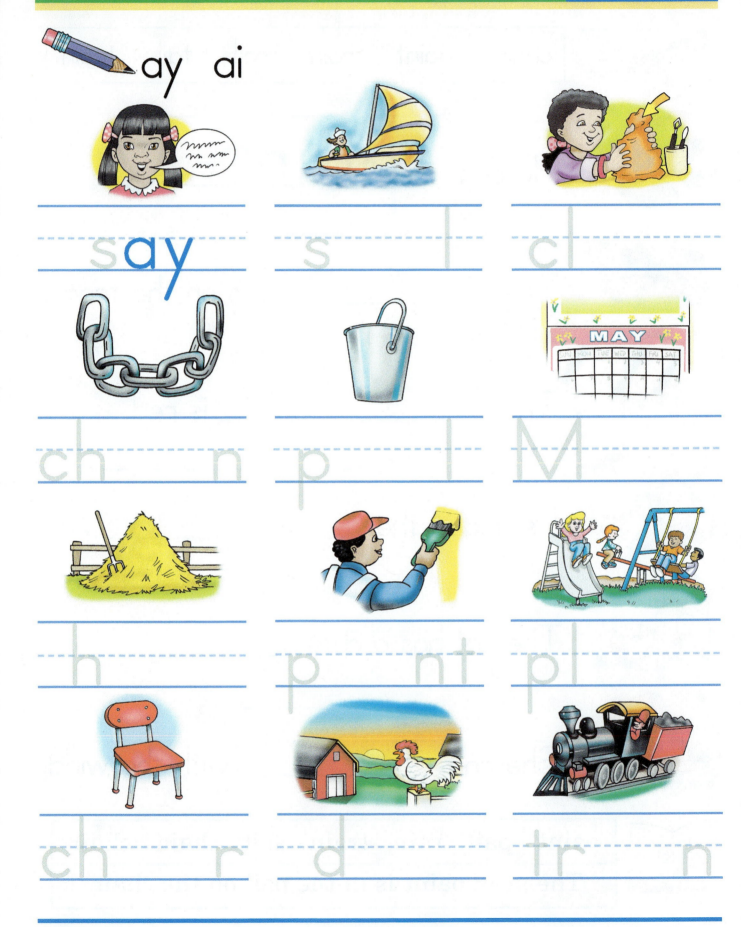

s __ay__

s __

c __

ch __

n __

p __

l __

M __

h __

p __

nt __

pl __

ch __

r __

d __

tr __

n __

oa   oe   ow

snow   c _ _ t   _ _ r

_ _ t   _ _ t   _ _ s p

h _ _   gr _ _   r _ _ d

_ _ b   _ _ f   bl _ _

boat	coat	crow	float	goat	row

This is my _____ coat .

The _____ is in the sea.

The _____ is black.

The _____ is on the grass.

He can _____ the boat.

I can _____ on my back.

row	road	rode	robe	toe	toad	hoe	home

Row the boat.   Throw the hoe in the hole in the road.

oo ou ew ue

new

p _ _ l

b l _ _

s p _ _ n

b l _ _

s _ _ p

b _ _ t

y _ _

f l _ _

t _ _ th

z _ _

g r _ _

| drew | glue | grew | moon | soup | stool |

The plant **grew** .

Sit on the _____ .

I eat _____ with a spoon.

The _____ is on the desk.

The _____ is in the sky.

I _____ a blue boot.

| blue | flew | flute | soup | pool | rule | drew | dune |

You threw the new blue tube in the pool.

ai ay ew oa oe oo ou ow ue

b **oa** t   b ___ t   h ___

s ___ p   s ___ p   gr ___

 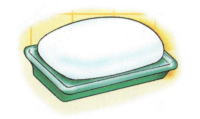 

gr ___   bl ___   bl ___

 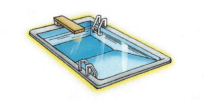

p ___ p   p ___ p   cl ___

– a

– i

– e

– a

– o

– a

old	fold	roll	bolt	blind	child
cold	hold	toll	colt	find	wild

colt

old   cold   colt   bolt   find   kind   child   wild

The roll is cold. The child is kind. The colt is wild.

car	star	bark	barn	arm	harp
jar	card	park	yarn	farm	smart

barn

car	cart	card	far	farm	arm	bark	barn

The car is in the barn on the farm. The park is dark.

bird	shirt	herd	corn	fork	curl
skirt	short	fern	horn	north	turn

herd

skirt shirt short fern turn corn herd hurt

The girl is short. The bird is hurt. Stir the corn.

ar er ir or ur

b **ir** d

b ___ n   n ___ c ___ n

g ___ l   t ___ n ___ n   n ___ th

sh ___ k   f ___ n   sk ___ t

h ___ d   h ___ t   st ___

DICTIONARY
pages 142–144

\- e

\- c

\- l

\- f

\- e

\- d

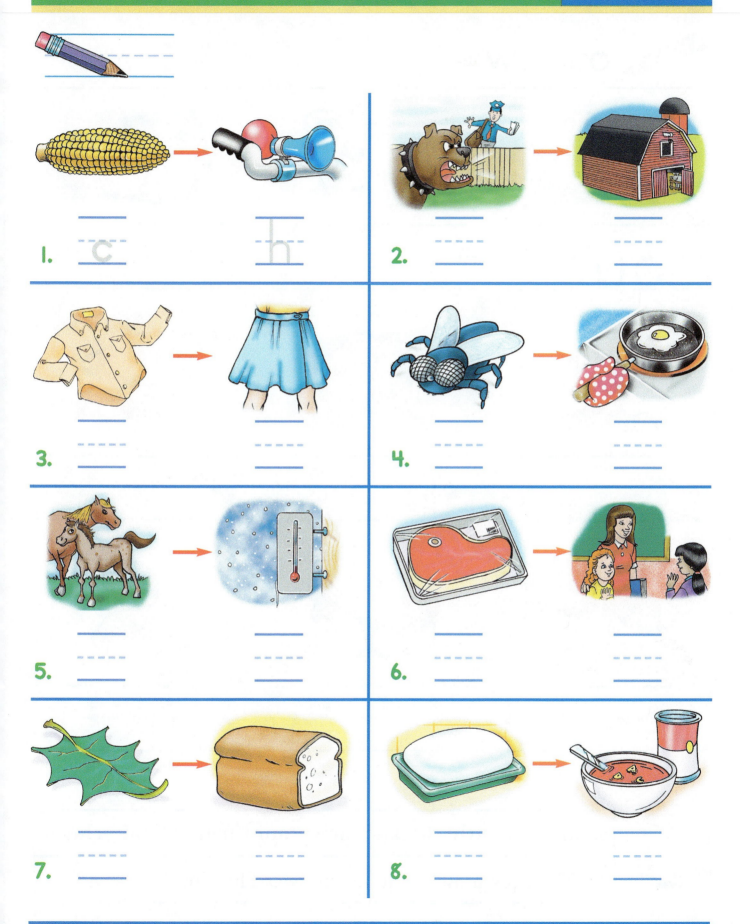

1. c   h

2.

3.

4.

5.

6.

7.

8.

ou   ow

house   c ___ ___   c l ___ ___ d

c l ___ n   m ___ ___ se   r ___ ___ nd

br ___ n   d ___ n   sh ___ t

mouse   mouth   house   how   our   owl   cloud   clown

The brown owl is in our house. The cloud is round.

| cloud | clown | cow | flour | mouse | round |

1. plow

COW

2. blouse

3. crown

4. proud

5. sour

6. found

oi oy

coin

b

b

l

t

p nt

s l

f l

boy   boil   toy   foil   Roy   soil   point

The coin is on the toy. The oil is in the soil.

aw au o

dog

dr___

s___ng

s___ce

___ff

s___

___ng

P___l

saw   say   dog   doll   off   on   draw   drew

Paul sang a long song. Draw the dog you saw.

| ball | call | fall | small | tall | wall |

The boy is ___tall___.

I see a big _____.

The dog is _____.

When did he _____?

We rake in the _____.

The clock is on the _____.

| ball | bag | call | cape | hall | hole | wall | well |

The wall is tall. The small ball is in the hall.

door   floor   oar   pour   score   store

Clean the _floor_.

She is in the _____.

The _____ is brown.

Row with the _____.

I can _____ the milk.

The _____ is four-four.

store   stool   pour   pond   roar   road   oar   our

The oar is on the floor in the store. Roar the score.

| book | bush | full | hook | put | took |

He __took__ the toy.

Read the _____ .

He is _____ .

The cap is on the _____ .

She _____ it on the shelf.

The _____ is green.

| book | moon | pull | rule | bull | mule | took | tooth |

Push and pull the door. Look at the bull in the brook.

bright	eight	light	taught
brought	eighty	night	thought
caught	high	sleigh	weight

high

eight   weight   weigh   high   light   thought   taught

She caught the ball and brought it home at night.

1   (2)   (1)   2   1   2   1   2

1   2   1   2   1   2   1   2

1   2   1   2   1   2   1   2

1   2   1   2   1   2   1   2

1   2   1   2   1   2   1   2

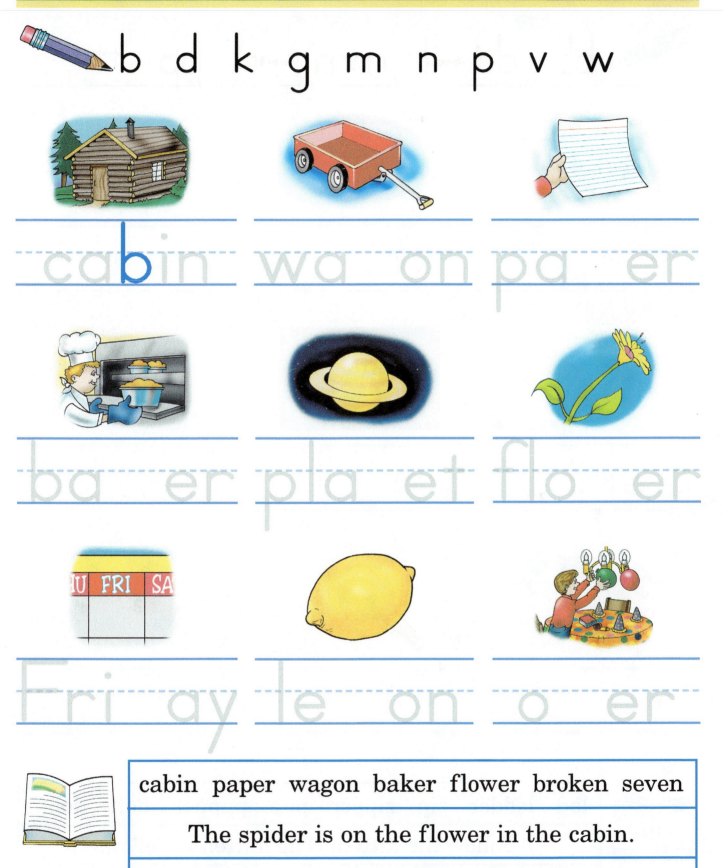

b d k g m n p v w

cabin   wa on   pa er

ba er   pla et   flo er

Fri ay   le on   o er

cabin paper wagon baker flower broken seven

The spider is on the flower in the cabin.

The crayon is broken.   The wagon is a present.

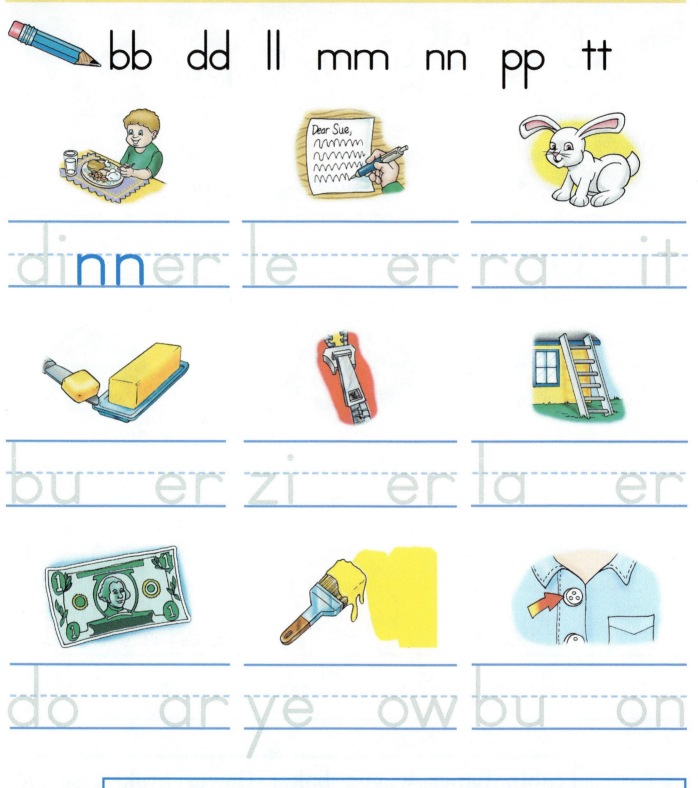

bb dd ll mm nn pp tt

di**nn**er   le___er   ra___it

bu___er   zi___er   la___er

do___ar   ye___ow   bu___on

lad ladder zip zipper pup puppet doll dollar

Follow the kitten. The mitten is yellow.

The zipper on the pillow is broken.

178

kitten	mitten	pillow	summer
ladder	muffin	puppet	

The kitten is cute.

We swim in the _____ .

I ate a _____ .

The _____ is on the bed.

The _____ is on my hand.

The _____ is blue.

The _____ is on the house.

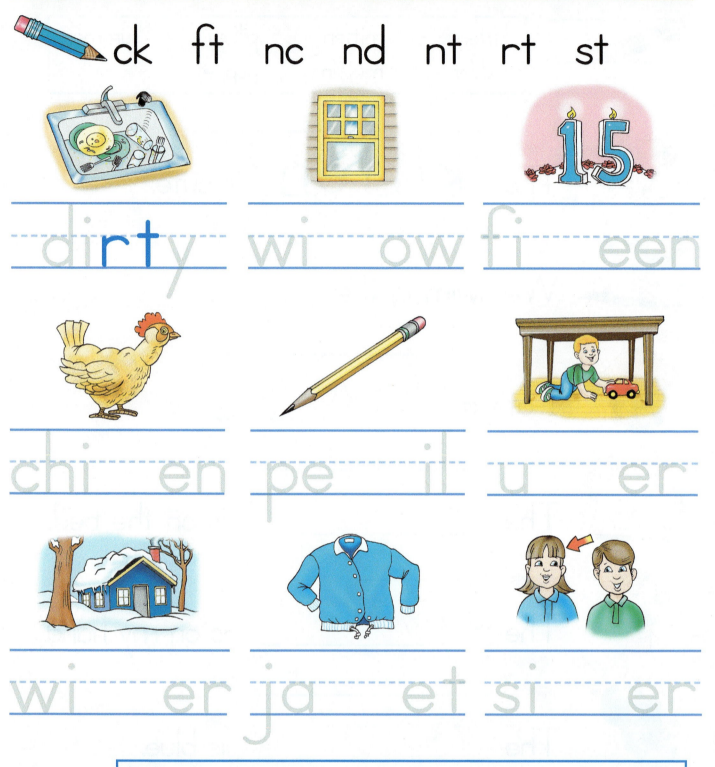

ck ft nc nd nt rt st

di**r**ty   wi__ow   fi__een

chi__en   pe__il   u__er

wi__er   ja__et   si__er

pen pencil sun Sunday win window fin finger

The jacket is dirty. The pencil is under the blanket.

My sister is angry. My father is on the tractor.

angry   blanket   doctor   father   finger   pencil   sister

He is my _father_.

This is my _____.

She is _____.

I went to the _____.

I hurt my _____.

The _____ is blue.

She is my _____.

father   fifteen   finger   jacket   pencil   sister   tractor

The **tractor** is red.

My _____ is a barber.

The cricket is on my _____.

This number is _____.

My _____ is in the garden.

The _____ is on the carpet.

My _____ is in my locker.

head	honey	glove	heavy
bread	money	monkey	feather
thread	mother	Monday	sweater

heavy

mother mom honey home head hat feather father

The sweater is on the monkey. The shovel is heavy.

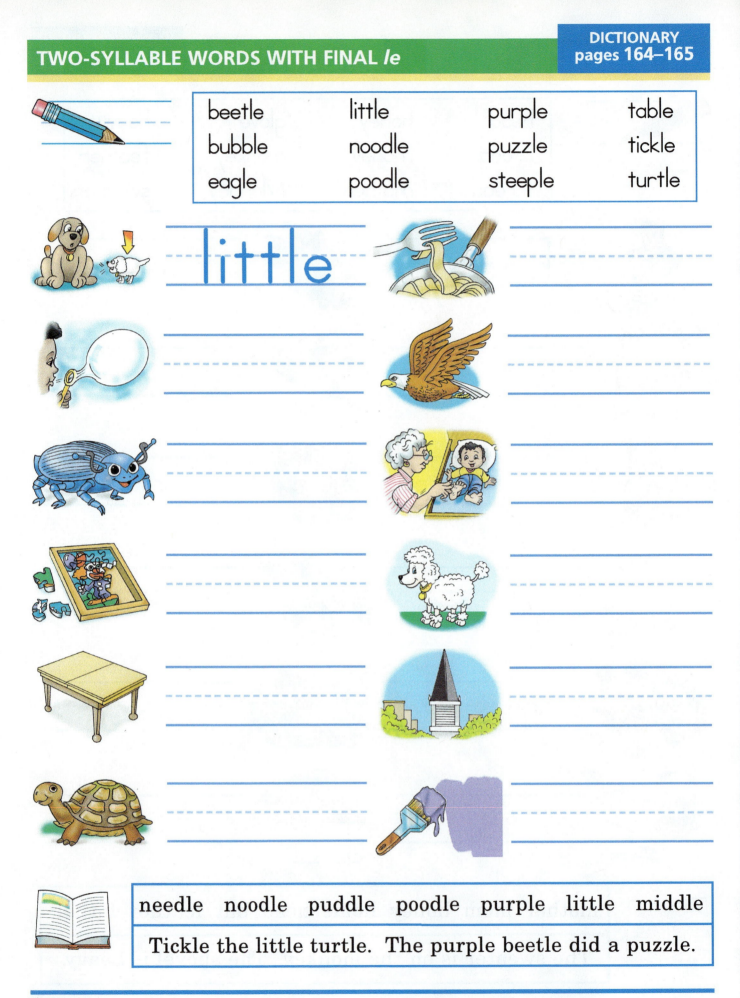

beetle	little	purple	table
bubble	noodle	puzzle	tickle
eagle	poodle	steeple	turtle

little

needle   noodle   puddle   poodle   purple   little   middle

Tickle the little turtle. The purple beetle did a puzzle.

apple   circle   cradle   eagle   needle   puddle   puzzle

The _eagle_ can fly.

The _____ is red.

The _____ is round.

The _____ is sharp.

She is in the _____.

The baby is in the _____.

Play with the _____.

eagle   little   middle   needle   purple   table   turtle

The _____eagle_____ is on the steeple.

The bottle is _____.

The candle is on the _____.

The purple marble is in the _____.

The pebble in my hand is _____.

The _____ is in the jungle.

The thimble is with the _____.

b h k l t w

wrist   ta k   nee

w ite   lam   lis en

rong   ca f   w ale

 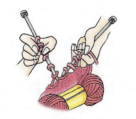 

com   nit   cas le

Climb   Knit   Knock   Talk   Wrap   Write

Knit a sweater.

the gift.

up high.

a letter.

on the door.

with me.

kit   knit   white   write   hall   half   list   listen

The lamb and the calf walk in the castle.

Listen, talk, and write with the white chalk.

s   es

pens   book   box

bike   globe   watch

seat   pencil   glass

maps   books   pens   rulers   brushes   watches

The books and the pencils are with the brushes.

The watches and the rulers are on the seats.

The maps and the globes are in the boxes.

brother's   clown's   puppet's   toad's
cat's   needle's   sister's

My __sister's__ bow is red.

My _____ backpack is heavy.

The _____ hat is little.

The _____ tail is long.

The _____ skin is brown.

The _____ tip is sharp.

The _____ shirt is blue and green.

leaf

loaf

fly

penny

wolf

shelf

leaves

fly flies leaf leaves half halves penny pennies

The babies play with the calves and the puppies.

The elves put the loaves on the shelves.

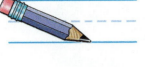

tooth

mouse

fish

teeth

sheep

woman

deer

foot feet mouse mice man men goose geese

The children see the geese, the mice, and the sheep.

The men and the women see the fish.

1. _____ ✔

2. _____ _____

3. _____ _____

4. _____ _____

5. _____ _____

6. _____ _____

7. _____ _____

8. _____ _____

9. _____ _____

10. _____ _____

scr spl spr str squ

street

ash

ay

ing

ing

are

eam

aw

atch

ring string spring lit split splash scratch

Splash in the spring. Stretch the string.

Scream at the squirrel in the street.

s   es

I cook and he ___cooks___.

I add and she _____.

We work and she _____.

I clean and he _____.

You play and she _____.

I brush and he _____.

| talk | talks | pull | pulls | push | pushes | itch | itches |

I cook and he cleans. She walks and he runs.

She pitches and he catches. Dad cleans the dishes.

ed

I **brushed** my teeth.

Mom _____.

Dad _____.

He _____ the floor.

She _____ on the slide.

She _____ with the chalk.

walk walked listen listened point pointed pitch pitched

You talked. I listened. He shouted. She yelled.

We pushed and pulled. She jumped. It crashed.

cooking   eating   playing   throwing
drawing   painting   singing

I'm **cooking** lunch.

She's _____ a ball.

He's _____ the wall.

We're _____ in the yard.

You're _____ a flower.

They're _____ a song.

It's _____ honey.

197

I'm   We're

1. We're singing.   2. _____ walking.

He's   She's

3. _____ working.   4. _____ sweeping.

It's   They're

5. _____ barking.   6. _____ playing.

| cried | dropped | raked | riding | running | sitting | writing |

He's __sitting__ at a desk.

We're _____ fast.

I'm _____ a letter.

The little boy _____.

She's _____ a bike.

You _____ the ball.

He _____ the leaves.

dries   flapped   fried   hiking   knitting   wiped   wrapped

I **wrapped** the gift.

My brother _____ the dishes.

My sister _____ the table.

She's _____ with the yarn.

We're _____ on the path.

My father _____ the egg.

The bird _____ its wings.

A <u>teacher</u> can teach.

A _____ can sing.

A _____ can bake.

A _____ can swim.

A _____ can paint.

An _____ can act.

farmer   conductor   baker   shopper   jogger   winner

My teacher is a good singer, dancer, and actor.

This swimmer is the winner. That jogger is a conductor.

| busy | cheese | hose | these | has |
| easy | choose | rose | those | |

rose

those   bees   has   flies   peas   is   easy   busy

Please close the door. My nose smells a rose.

The cheese has holes. Choose these, not those.

g gh ph

phone

__iant

___oto

__ar_e

_tau___

dol__in

cou___

__iraffe

gra__

phone alphabet graph laugh giant orange photo

The dolphin and the elephant laugh at the giraffe.

The giant is large.   The phone is orange.

come   have   said   was
give   none   some   were

was

Come home. Give me a dime.

This dog has some bones. That dog has none.

The painter said some paint was in the pail.

Save the pennies you have. We were wet.

DICTIONARY pages 180–181

black	circle	pink	triangle
blue	gray	red	white
brown	green	square	yellow

red

The cow is brown and white. The whale is black and gray.

My shirt is blue and red. The circle is round.

| black | green | oval | rectangle | square |
| circle | orange | purple | red | triangle |

Colors

Shapes

black

circle

book	chalk	glove	pencil
boot	desk	jacket	shirt
chair	globe	paper	skirt

desk

Put the book, the pencil, and the crayon on the desk.

The doll has a skirt, a sweater, sneakers, and a hat.

book	cap	crayon	doll	hat
boot	coat	desk	dress	yo-yo

Objects & Toys

Clothing

book

boot

apple	corn	lemon	nut
cake	egg	meat	pea
cheese	ham	milk	rice

nut

We're eating meat, rice, beans, noodles, and bread.

I'm baking muffins with flour, butter, and honey.

? ?

| boot | cake | coat | glove | hat |
| butter | cap | fig | ham | pea |

Clothing

Food

boot

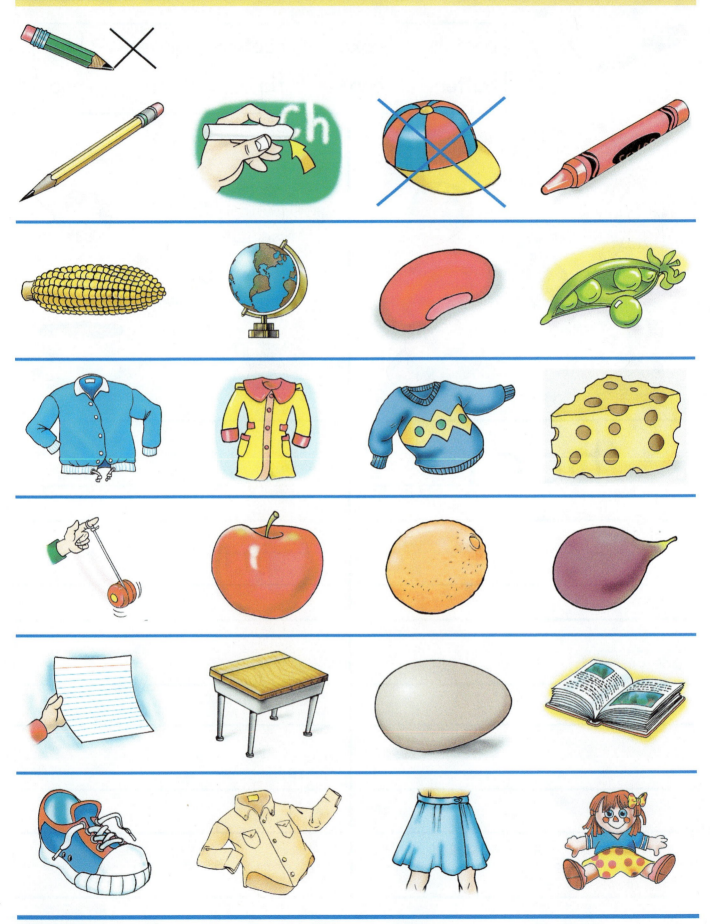

bee	cow	flower	owl
boy	crow	goat	sheep
camel	eagle	jay	skunk

boy

The bee is on the flower. The ant is on the rose.

The girl and boy see a rabbit and a skunk in a bush.

_?_ _?_

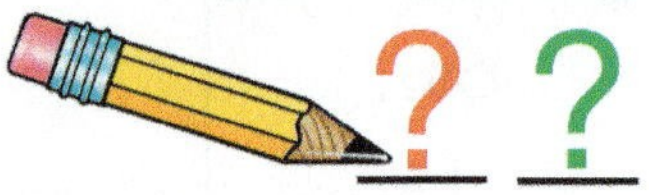

| crow | eagle | goat | monkey | rabbit |
| duck | fox | jay | owl | skunk |

Animals

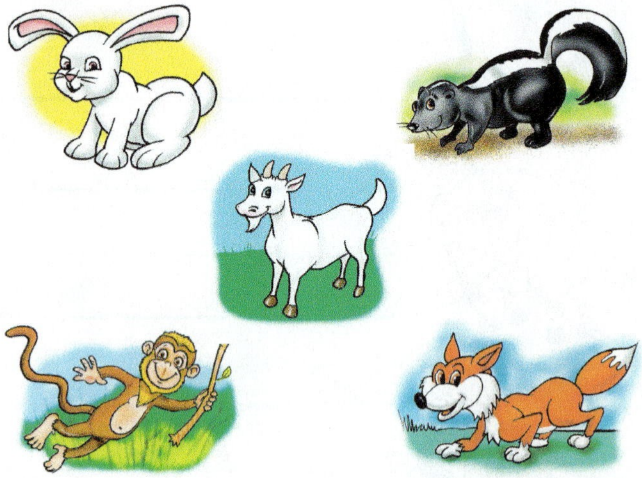

Birds

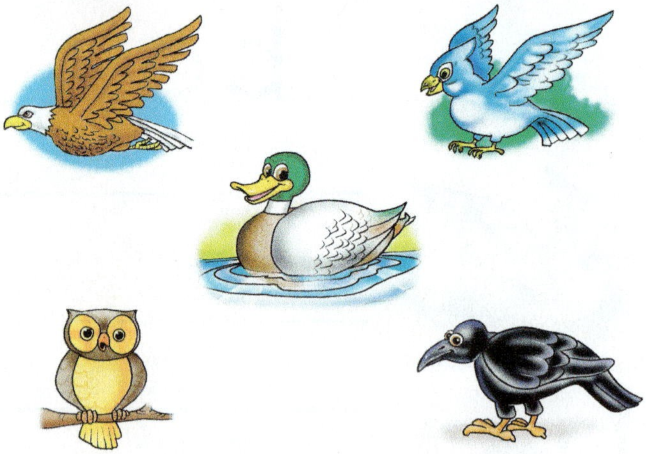

crow

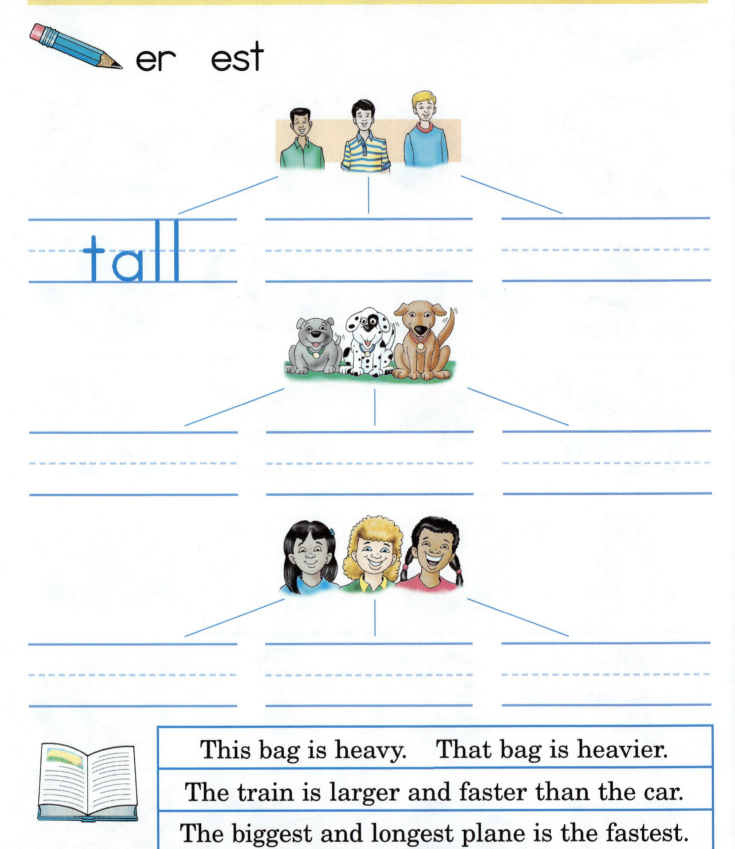

er   est

tall

This bag is heavy.   That bag is heavier.

The train is larger and faster than the car.

The biggest and longest plane is the fastest.

Monday was hotter and windier than Sunday.

ship

sad

large

bunny

unhappy

rabbit

big

boat

small

present

song

store

shop

little

tune

gift

Shut the big door. Close the large window.

Sing a song in the shop. Play a tune in the store.

Give a small present. Give a little gift.

day
night

new
old

push
pull

over
under

right
left

last
first

night

Push it up. Pull it down. Open it. Close it.

The day was hot and the night was cold.

The big car is new. The little car is old.

new	last	short	dirty
first	over	open	tall
left	old	clean	close
under	night	high	heavy
day	right	light	low
push	happy	give	large
cold	over	long	summer
sad	hot	winter	rest
up	down	small	take
under	pull	work	short

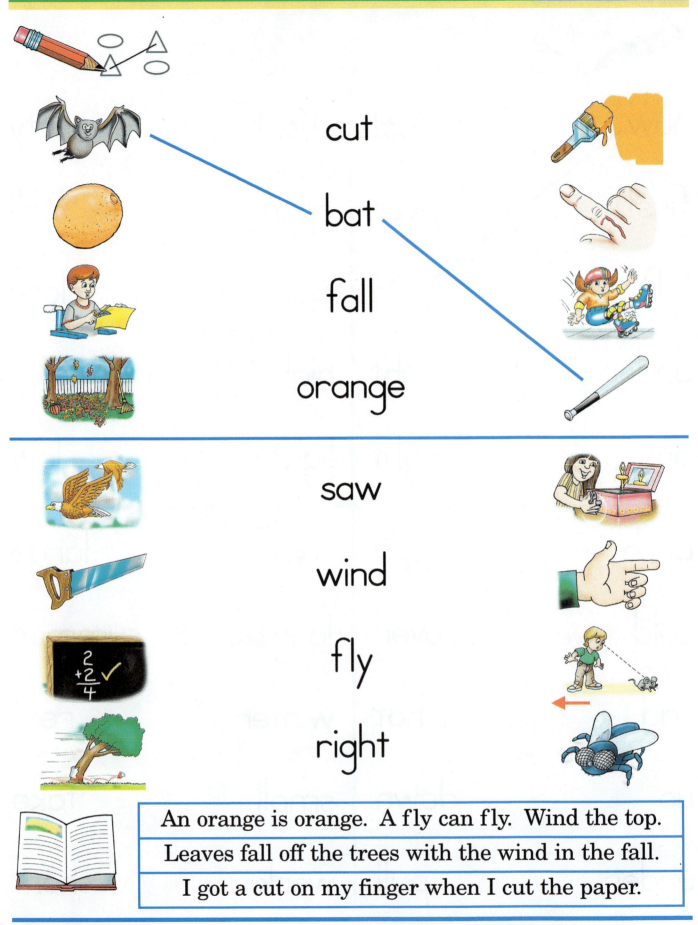

cut

bat

fall

orange

saw

wind

fly

right

An orange is orange. A fly can fly. Wind the top.

Leaves fall off the trees with the wind in the fall.

I got a cut on my finger when I cut the paper.

right

(write)

meet

meat

flour

flower

eight

ate

wrap

rap

sea

see

ate

eight

see

sea

meet

meat

right

write

flour

flower

wrap

rap

We meet and rap. Wrap the meat.

I see eight flowers in the sea. The mouse ate the flour.

We rode on the road. I write with my right hand.

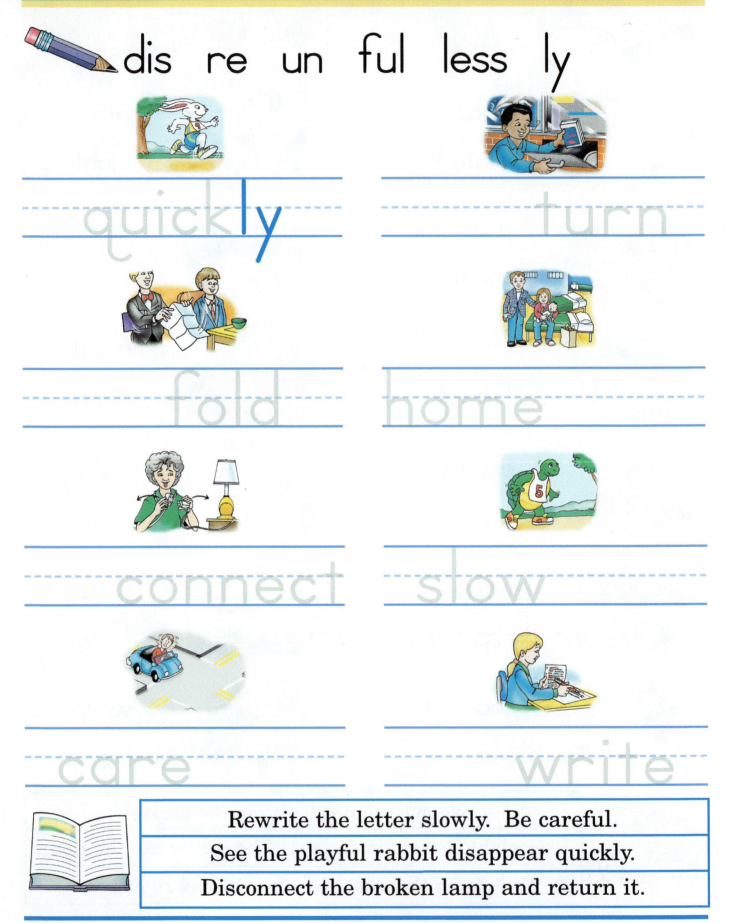

dis re un ful less ly

quickly

turn

fold

home

connect

slow

care

write

Rewrite the letter slowly. Be careful.

See the playful rabbit disappear quickly.

Disconnect the broken lamp and return it.

disappear   quickly   slowly   weightless
playful   rewrite   unhappy

The rabbit hops quickly .

The kitten is _____ .

Please _____ it.

See the bunny _____ .

The turtle walks _____ .

She is _____ .

In space she is _____ .

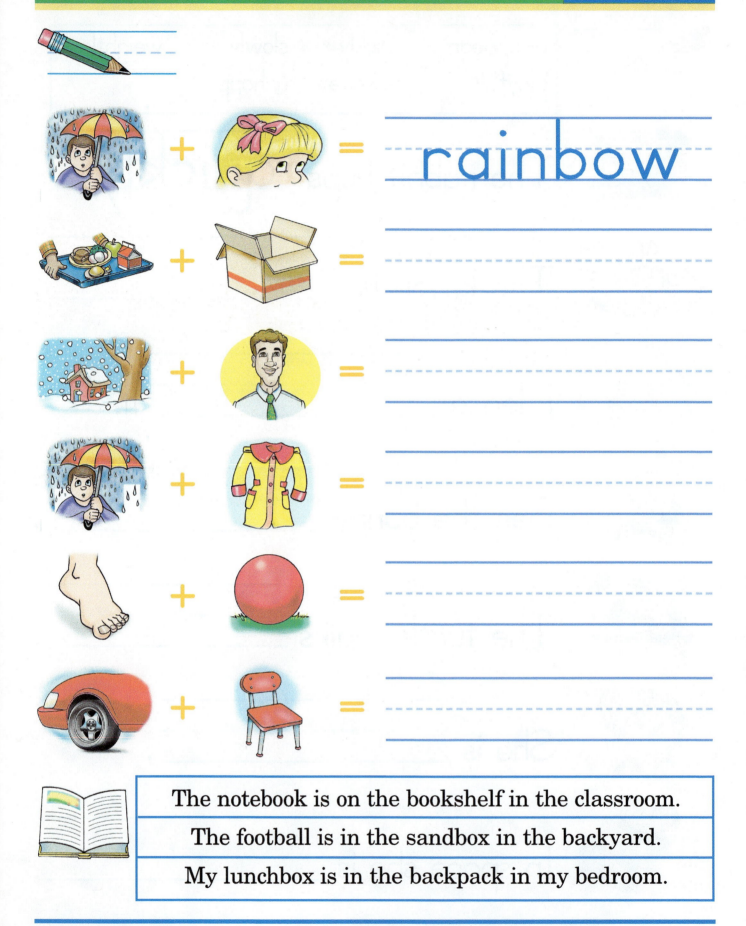

= **rainbow**

The notebook is on the bookshelf in the classroom.

The football is in the sandbox in the backyard.

My lunchbox is in the backpack in my bedroom.

| rainbow | sandbox | skateboard | swingset | treehouse |

My little sister is in the <u>sandbox</u>.

My older sister is on the _____.

My brother is riding his _____.

My father is fixing our _____.

My mother is looking at the _____.

227

1 2 3 4 5

3
___   ___   ___   ___

___   ___   ___   ___

___   ___   ___   ___

___   ___   ___   ___

A grasshopper and a dragonfly met a caterpillar.

The strawberry yogurt is in the refrigerator.

The alligator and the hippopotamus talked with the kangaroo and the porcupine.

grasshopper   kangaroo   octopus   woodpecker

hippopotamus   newspaper   strawberry   xylophone

The _octopus_ is reading the _____.

The _____ is eating a _____.

The _____ is playing the _____.

The _____ is sitting on the _____.

229

big

(little)

chair

desk

shop

boat

print

paint

write

right

right

left

penny

pennies

cheese

choose

spring

string

soap

soup

tub

tube

shirt

skirt

sea

see

mouse

mice

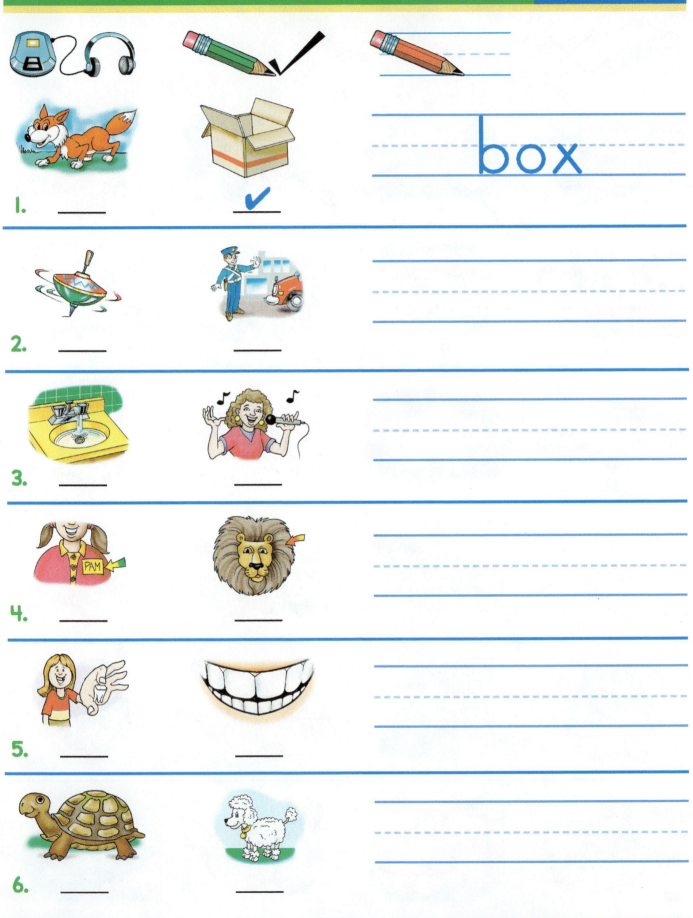

1. _____   ✔

box

2. _____   _____

3. _____   _____

4. _____   _____

5. _____   _____

6. _____   _____

? ?

bean	cheese	monkey	sheep
boot	coat	orange	sneaker
boy	girl	rabbit	woman

Clothing

Food

bean

Animals

People

LISTENING SCRIPTS

PAGE 21
Listen and choose the correct picture.
1. pit
2. zip
3. bat
4. cap
5. pig
6. van

PAGE 36
Listen and choose the correct picture.
1. pin
2. get
3. jug
4. hen
5. fog
6. run

PAGE 37
Listen and choose the correct picture.
1. pig
2. can
3. map
4. bug
5. hot
6. cat

PAGE 42
Listen and choose the correct picture.
1. can
2. ham
3. mat
4. rap
5. bad
6. tap
7. bat
8. sad

PAGE 55
Listen and choose the correct picture.
1. odd
2. ill
3. egg
4. add
5. up
6. on

PAGE 58
Listen and choose the correct picture.
1. mud
2. mom
3. nut
4. net
5. man
6. met

PAGE 61
Listen and choose the correct picture.
1. set
2. fan
3. sit
4. fog
5. sun
6. sell

PAGE 64
Listen and choose the correct picture.
1. hit
2. hog
3. job
4. jug
5. ham
6. hug

PAGE 67
Listen and choose the correct picture.
1. log
2. run
3. lip
4. lap
5. red
6. rod

PAGE 70
Listen and choose the correct picture.
1. pet
2. bat
3. pin
4. pup
5. big
6. beg

PAGE 73
Listen and choose the correct picture.
1. tag
2. dig
3. top
4. ten
5. dip
6. tug

PAGE 76
Listen and choose the correct picture.
1. get
2. cub
3. cat
4. gum
5. got
6. kid

PAGE 92
Listen and choose the correct picture.
1. ran
2. spin
3. lap
4. spot
5. slip
6. top
7. flip
8. clap
9. frog
10. flat

PAGE 100
Listen and choose the correct picture.
1. wind
2. wet
3. fist
4. band
5. net
6. went
7. sad
8. vest
9. list
10. lift

PAGE 115
Listen and choose the correct picture.
1. bring
2. wing
3. sting
4. thing
5. rang
6. fang

PAGE 117
Listen and choose the correct picture.
1. bank
2. stink
3. blink
4. drank
5. think
6. sink

PAGE 118
Listen and choose the correct picture.
1. rink
2. sing
3. wing
4. think
5. bank
6. thank
7. sting
8. drink
9. blank
10. stink

PAGE 140
Listen and choose the correct picture.
1. cape
2. tube
3. cut
4. pine
5. tap
6. mane
7. kite
8. can
9. note
10. cube

PAGE 193
Listen and choose the correct picture.
1. bikes
2. glass
3. puppies
4. mice
5. tooth
6. leaf
7. feet
8. book
9. pens
10. men

PAGE 232
Listen and choose the correct picture.
1. box
2. stop
3. sink
4. name
5. teeth
6. turtle

(A complete Answer Key for this workbook may be found in the *Word by Word Primary* Teacher's Guide.)

A B C D E F G H I

J K L M N O P Q R

S T U V W X Y Z

a b c d e f g h i

j k l m n o p q r

s t u v w x y z

WORKBOOK ACTIVITY INSTRUCTIONS KEY

	Read (silently and aloud). Practice individually, with a partner, and as a class.
	Write.
	Choose the correct letter(s). to complete the word.
or	Choose the correct answer. (Put a circle or oval around it.)
	Choose the correct answer. Then write the word.
	Listen and choose the correct answer.
	Listen and put a check under the correct picture.
	Listen and put a check under the correct picture. Later, write a word for each picture you checked.
	Put an X on the picture that doesn't belong with the others.
	Draw a line to match the item on the left with the correct item on the right.
	Write each word from the box under the correct category.

Give children the opportunity to hear and say all words in all activities throughout this workbook. Children can do the activities silently in school or at home and then practice saying the words aloud as a class, with another child, or with a tutor, aide, parent, or other adult.